THE EMMITT ZONE

Ryan

THE EMMITT ZONE™

EMMITT SMITH

with Steve Delsohn

Taylor Publishing Company   Dallas, Texas

Published by Taylor Publishing Company
1550 West Mockingbird Lane
Dallas, Texas 75235

Reprinted by arrangement with Crown Publishers, Inc.

Library of Congress Cataloging-in-Publication Data

Smith, Emmitt, 1969–
    The Emmitt zone / Emmitt Smith with Steve Delsohn.
      p.   cm.
    Originally published: New York : Crown Publishers, ©1994.
    Includes index.
    ISBN 0-87833-920-5
    1. Smith, Emmitt, 1969– . 2. Football players—United States—
Biography. 3. Dallas Cowboys (Football team)—History.
I. Delsohn, Steve. II. Title.
[GV939.S635A3   1995]
796.332'092—dc20
[B]   95-33136
                                           CIP

Printed in the United States of America

10 9 8 7 6 5 4 3 2 1

September 1995

This book is dedicated to my family for providing a loving, nurturing environment that ensured the foundation for my success; to young people everywhere . . . dreams do come true; and to the Lord above who makes all things possible.

—E.S.

For Vaughn M. Anthony—father, husband, fighter until the end. May God bless you and keep you.

—S.D.

CONTENTS

CONTENTS

ACKNOWLEDGMENTS

I could never thank all of the people who contributed to my success on and off the field. I would like to acknowledge the following individuals for their respective roles in my life.

To my mother for her unconditional love, nurturing, and positive impact on my life, and to my father, my first football hero, for his guidance.

My late grandmother Erma L. Smith and my grandfather Emmitt J. Smith, Sr., for their wisdom and teachings.

To my sisters and brothers, Marsha, Connie, Erik, Emil, and Emory, for their ongoing love, support, and friendship.

My high school coach, Dwight Thomas, for providing me with my first opportunity to experience competitive football.

The University of Florida, my teammates, coaches, students, fans, and alumni for providing me with one of the best times and educational experiences of my life.

My fraternity brothers, Phi Beta Sigma, for showing me the meaning of brotherhood.

My Cowboy teammates, coaches, and administration, who I must thank for allowing me to be successful on the field during my professional career to date.

My management team for steering me in the right direction off the field. My attorney, the General, Mike Ferguson for his relentless attention to detail, loyalty, and commitment. My agent, Richard Howell, for his patience in contract negotiations.

My marketing consultant, Werner Scott, of Advantage Marketing Group (AMG) for his strategic vision, and Larry Lundy along with the rest of the AMG team for making things happen.

And finally Steve Delsohn, my co-writer, Frank Weimann, my literary agent, and Jane Cavolina of Crown Publishers, for bringing my thoughts to print.

—E.S.

For their generous help and support, thanks to Frank Weimann, Scott Waxman, Jane Cavolina, Dakila Divina, Shari Wenk, David Rubenstein, Brian Peterson, Werner Scott, Larry Lundy, Lynn Conway, Mike Ferguson, Harriette Peebles, Cheryl Booth, Tricia and Joe Robinson, and Emma and Mary Kay Delsohn.

—S.D.

ACKNOWLEDGMENTS

THE EMMITT ZONE

1
WHATEVER IT TAKES

iants Stadium. New York against Dallas. Sunday, January 2, 1994. A cold, tense, punishing afternoon of professional football. Just before halftime, I burst through a hole on the right and start motoring toward the end zone. Forty-six yards later, safety Greg Jackson slams me to the artificial turf. I'm rolling around in pain. My shoulder is separated.

Up until I got hurt, we were leading New York 10–0 in a game that was huge for both teams. The sixteenth and final game of the regular season, its winner would gain the National Football Conference East title, a bye the following week, and home field advantage throughout the playoffs. The losers that day would also make the playoffs. But they'd enter as the wild card, and frequently this means trouble. It's always harder to win the Super Bowl from the road.

Going into that final Sunday, I was also chasing my third straight rushing title, something only three players in history had ever accomplished. My first rushing title was probably the sweetest, but this year there was a twist. A very personal twist. Back in September, in the midst of a contract dispute with Jerry Jones, I had sat out our first two games. And in my opinion, Jerry had openly questioned my value to the Cowboys.

But that was just talk. The only statement I needed to make was on the football field, and I felt I could make it loudest by overcoming the odds: In the history of the NFL, no runner had missed two games and still won the rushing title.

With more than 100 yards before it was halftime, I was on the verge in New York when I got injured.

It happened on my longest gain of the day. Late in the second quarter, I ran through an enormous hole inside our right tackle, put a move on the safety racing at me from inside, then turned the right corner and headed north and south. But this was my nineteenth carry in just the first half, my legs didn't have their usual strength, and I'm not known for my world-class speed to begin with. Making my way downfield, I couldn't pull away from their other safety, Greg Jackson.

As I saw him about to catch me, I protected the ball

with the left side of my body, while breaking my fall with my right. Jackson's hit was only routine, but it pushed me down hard on my right elbow. Then Jackson's body weight fell on my elbow too. As the pain shot up to my shoulder, I immediately knew I was injured. My entire right arm felt dead and I couldn't move it.

Even when I'm not hurt, I tend to get up slowly. It's something my father taught me my rookie year. He told me, "Son, lay down on that ground until everyone else gets off you. Don't waste all your energy pushing that weight off your back. Reserve some of that energy for the next play."

It was sound advice and I still follow it today, but this time I had no choice. For a moment or two, the pain was so sharp it kept me pinned to the turf. I didn't stay there too long, though. Not with all the Giants staring at me.

As I went to the sideline, some of the feeling returned to my right arm. So with just two minutes left until half-time—when they could better evaluate the damage—I only sat out two plays before trotting back to our huddle. The instant the New York fans saw this, they let out a groan. I didn't take any offense, though. With so much on the line for both teams that afternoon, I saw it instead as a sign of their respect.

Troy Aikman threw two completions just before half-time, and an Eddie Murray field goal put us ahead 13–0. I headed straight for our training room, where our trainer helped me out of my shoulder pads and our doctor took X rays.

My shoulder was separated, they told me a few minutes later. They called it a "grade-two," which is worse than grade-one, but not as severe as grade-three. In a grade-three, they explained, they'd already be able to see a deformity in the shoulder. I didn't have that, they said.

All in all I thought it was decent news. At least nothing got broken.

"So what are my options?" I asked them.

First they could tape and Ace-bandage the shoulder. Then, to cushion some of the blows, they could tape a knee pad on top of the bandage. I told them, "Do it, do it," but our trainer gave me a warning before they got started.

He said, "Emmitt, it's gonna hurt like hell when you get hit. You're gonna have to work through it. Now, we want you to go, but if you feel like you can't, we understand."

I said, "Fine. I want to see what I can do."

In a league as violent as ours, a lot of people play hurt. I wanted to be a guy who could play hurt and still be effective.

But you want to know the real truth? It wasn't all about playing hurt. At that point at least, it wasn't even all about helping us win; with a 13-point lead, I felt we already had the game in hand. So the main reason I kept playing was to win my third consecutive rushing title. Along with our team repeating as Super Bowl champs, this was my season-long mission. And injured shoulder or not, I felt I was too close now to simply quit.

My motivation changed almost immediately.

By the time they finished working on my shoulder, it was early in the third quarter and the Giants were punting. As I walked out of our tunnel and onto the field, I saw our return man fumble the punt. Then I saw the bodies unpile and the Giants recover the ball at our 39. They banged right in for a touchdown to make it 13–7, and suddenly we were fighting for this ball game.

From that moment on, I never even considered the rushing title. I was just out there to win.

My first second-half carry, my twentieth of the game, was a beautiful thing. We ran a toss to the right, and I picked up about 9 yards before running out of room along the sideline. I recall thinking: I didn't even get hit! I sure hope the whole second half is like this.

I got a grip on myself the very next play, the exact same toss but over to the left. This time I cut inside, into pursuit, and one of the New York linebackers bashed my shoulder. I told myself through the pain: You're playing against the Giants, you stupid fool. Did you really think they'd let you off that easy?

Actually, my teammates and I don't hate the Giants as much as we hate the Philadelphia Eagles. But like the Eagles, the Giants are always physical. They play the game hard, not fancy, and any team like that has my respect.

That year, New York's defense ranked first in giving up fewest points. And as the wind and cold set in during the second half, our yardage was getting harder to come by. At the end of the third quarter, we still hadn't scored since halftime, and the Giants had just kicked a field goal. That made it 13–10 Cowboys, with one quarter to go in the regular season.

Those next fifteen minutes were hell. Every fourth-quarter shot I took, the pain grew more intense. One time I caught a pass out of the backfield, tried to fake out a Giant, and he didn't bite. As he hit me and I went down, my upper body got smashed between him and the frozen ground, and I heard a pop inside my chest. This was injury number two, and I heard it again a few plays later, that ugly crackling sound.

Once again our offense had not moved the football, so our punting team came in and I walked to the sideline. Jimmy Johnson walked up to me, looking concerned. By that point in the game, my right arm was just dangling there by my side.

Jimmy said, "Emmitt, are you okay? Do you wanna go? Just tell me if you can't, because we'll put Lincoln in there."

Jimmy meant Lincoln Coleman, my 245-pound backup. Lincoln Coleman can play; everyone on the Dallas Cowboys knows that. But there was no way I was sitting down now. I was into this thing too deep.

I told Jimmy, "Just keep an eye on me and have Lincoln ready to come. I'm gonna go as far as I can."

About midway through the fourth quarter, the score still 13–10 Dallas, Rodney Hampton took over. Even before he became a star in New York, I always knew Rodney could play. Back in the Southeastern Conference, Rodney was running the ball at Georgia while I was at Florida. Today people mostly talk about Rodney's physical side, and there is no question that Rodney can lower the hammer. But he also makes people miss, catches passes, and blocks.

On this particular drive Rodney was running, and running, and running, and I have to admit he was ticking me off. It wasn't anything personal, of course. But nothing torments me more than standing on my own sideline, feeling helpless, watching the clock run down while the other running back dominates the game. I want to be the man when the spotlight is on.

With ten seconds left and the Giants down 3, Rodney carried the ball to our 14. Their field goal team ran out and the New York crowd groaned again. With time for one more pass play, they wanted Giants coach Dan Reeves to go for the winning touchdown, not for the tying field goal.

As for myself, I felt relieved. Even if David Treadwell made the kick, we could still win in overtime. If Treadwell missed, we'd win right now and get the hell out of Dodge.

Unfortunately for us, Treadwell was good from 31 yards, and the Giants suddenly seemed to have the momentum. To tie the game at 13, they'd outscored us 13–0 in the second half. They also had the home crowd and the ball first in overtime.

When our defense came up big, making the Giants punt to our 25, the pressure fell on our offense, and I was telling myself as we ran back out there: "It's nothing but pain—just block out the pain."

When this much is at stake, normally I want the football. I want it badly. But with my shoulder killing me now, I didn't care if I carried at all. As long as we won.

So why did I even go out there? I felt that I had to, if only to pose the threat of the running game. As great a quarterback as Troy Aikman is—and I think Troy is the best in the league—he needs a runner like me to slow down the pass rush. Otherwise Troy would take a terrible beating, and so would our passing game.

I was much more than a threat, as things turned out.

THE EMMITT ZONE

On our next eleven plays in overtime, I handled the ball nine times, and gained 41 of our 51 yards. I wasn't happy that I carried such a large load. I wasn't unhappy, either. I was off by myself somewhere, some private zone, feeling too much pain to focus on anything else but winning.

The tension was thick in our huddle that final drive. Some guys were looking at Troy, waiting to hear the next play, but I also felt some of their eyes glancing at me. From the time I hurt my shoulder, my teammates had started asking me how I felt. I appreciated that, but now they were asking between almost every play, and hearing it over and over was frustrating me. So I mostly just kept my head down, clenching my fists and biting into my mouthpiece—until I bit right through it. Then Michael Irvin asked me again, "Emmitt, are you okay?" And that's when it all boiled over.

"Michael!" I yelled. "I'm fine! Leave me alone!"

Michael said, "No, I'm gonna ask you every play. Every play, just so you know I'm there. I'm there, man, okay?"

Looking back on it now, that moment in New York epitomized Mike Irvin. Beneath all the flash, the man is solid and pure.

On one of my final carries, I stiff-armed Lawrence Taylor with my bad right arm. I did it purely on instinct, and it hurt me far more than it hurt him, but it did buy us some yards. It also gave me some payback. A few years before, with no provocation at all, the man slugged me in the face. I don't think Lawrence did it intentionally. I don't know *how* he did it. But I was running and he was closing in, and boom, he put that big fist of his right through my face mask. At the time it stung my nose and watered my eyes, but now I'm glad it happened. How many guys can say they got punched by L.T.?

On another carry that drive, I got hit by two Giants simultaneously, and I heard that crack again inside my chest. I went out for one play, came back in and gained 10 more yards, saw we were in field goal range, and looked toward the sideline: Hey, get me outta here!

Jimmy sent out the field goal team. Eddie "Money" Murray slammed it through from 41 yards. The New York crowd fell dead silent. I never saw Eddie make his game-winning kick, though. I was curled up on our bench, tears in my eyes. Tears of pain and emotion.

At first, I actually felt pretty good in our locker room. But after I showered and partially dressed, the pain advanced again. It was chest spasms this time, chest spasms so intense I couldn't move. I just sat there in front of my locker, trying to breathe.

They carried me back to the training room, propped me up on a table, cut me out of my shirt, and packed my chest with ice. When Michael Irvin walked in and hugged me around the neck, my eyes filled up again. I don't know what I was feeling then. Friendship, victory, pain—probably all of it.

Michael left and John Madden appeared. He'd been broadcasting that day for CBS.

"My entire career," John Madden said, "I've never come down to the locker room. I came down today to shake your hand. I've never seen a better performance than that."

Although I was thinking, Wow, I only said, "Thank you."

A minute or two after John walked out, Jimmy Johnson

THE EMMITT ZONE

stopped in before addressing the media. Looking extremely excited about our huge win, he told me I did "a heck of a job." Then Jimmy patted me on my bad shoulder!

I just looked at him and said, "Thanks, Coach."

The moment he left I shouted, "More aspirin!"

When the pain calmed down again, I pulled myself together emotionally, put on some clothes, and went out to face the media. The reporters wanted to know what they figured the public would: Why did I stay in the game? How much pain was I in? How much of it was the rushing title, and did I have an incentive bonus for that?

I told them: No, I have no incentive clause in my contract. The rushing title was personal, not about dollars. And the moment the game got close, I never gave it another thought; I only wanted to win.

Before we left Giants Stadium, they had given me some painkilling medication. It knocked me out on the bus ride to Newark Airport, but once we boarded our plane I felt rotten again, so our medical staff suggested I sit in back with them. Ordinarily, I sit with Michael Irvin.

Even before we took off, the inside of my chest started to hammer. But this pain was farther left, close to my heart. It scared the hell out of me, and the doctors, too. They nearly decided to take me off the plane, check me into a hospital in New Jersey. When the pain eased again, they opted for more medication. This time it was a shot. Then the plane was up in the air and I was dreaming.

Though I didn't know it, my entire body was jerking as I slept. Then somewhere up above Memphis I woke in a panic.

EMMITT SMITH

"Do you want us to land this plane?" I heard somebody ask me.

And I heard my own voice say, "No. Just get me back to Dallas."

Later in the flight, Jimmy Johnson tried cheering me up. Addressing the team on our airplane's loudspeaker, he congratulated the Cowboys for winning the NFC East. "And congratulations to Emmitt Smith," Jimmy added. "Today he just won his third straight rushing title!"

Sitting up near the front with our other coaches, Jimmy somehow had just learned the news. With 168 yards against the Giants, and 1,486 for the season, I had beaten out the Los Angeles Rams' Jerome Bettis.

My teammates went crazy, especially our offensive linemen, since this rushing title belonged to those hosses too. I tried to enjoy it, but just before landing in Dallas, that hammering sensation returned to my chest. The doctor told me, "You don't have a choice. We're checking you into a hospital for the evening."

That night was a blur of pain pills, medicated IV, and prayer. In the morning they X-rayed my shoulder and chest. The chest X ray showed no breaks; I had only bruised my sternum and probably a couple of ribs. The shoulder X ray showed no further separation. This was a great relief. With twelve or thirteen days before our first playoff game, I felt that I would be ready. Maybe not 100 percent, but healthy enough to go.

Although the doctors released me, I never went home that Monday morning. I went straight to our training room instead, so they could start treating my shoulder. In the mirror, with my shirt off, the swelling on my right side caught me off guard. It covered my clavicle, my trap, part of my pectoral muscle, and even the heart of my biceps. I took one deep breath and turned away. No reason to freak myself out.

When I read the paper that afternoon, all my numbers were printed there: 168 yards rushing on 32 carries. Another 61 yards on pass receptions, for a total of 229. Of our team's 70 plays, I had handled the ball on 42. Seventeen of those came after I hurt my shoulder. So did 78 of my total yards.

For several more weeks, I would pay for those numbers with pain. And after the season ended, I would also undergo surgery on my right shoulder. But that's the NFL. When the cameras blink off and the fans go home, sometimes for players the drama is only beginning.

When I walked into my apartment that Monday evening, there were more than a dozen messages on my machine. It was mostly friends and some nonimmediate family, saying they'd never forget the performance I gave. Even today, people still walk up and tell me about that game. By the details they recall, I know they really saw it, and that feels nice.

But right after that game against the Giants, I really didn't think about it much. The playoffs were coming up fast, and we were the defending Super Bowl champs. This was no time to be satisfied.

EMMITT SMITH

2
JIMMY
JOHNSON

Unless you *truly* don't follow sports, you know Jimmy isn't with the Cowboys anymore. I'll talk about this later on, and I'll talk about some events that might have contributed. But I don't see any reason to get that serious now. Not when we can talk about Jimmy's hair.

Normally, this is exactly how I needle Jimmy about his hair: when he isn't around, but I know he'll find out anyway. Like the time I appeared on *Inside the NFL*, that great show on HBO, shortly after we'd won our first Super Bowl. In the game's final moments, I had messed up Jimmy's hair on national television. Then I'd kept on messing it up to make sure it actually moved.

Now, on HBO, Chris Collinsworth was saying to me: "I'm glad you didn't rub your hands in his hair before that game. You probably would have fumbled."

I said, "No, if I'd rubbed my hands in his hair before the game, I would probably *not* have fumbled, because Jimmy's hair is like stickum!"

I didn't always go through the media, though. Sometimes, at practice, I'd look at Jimmy with this expression of true alarm. Then I'd say, "Coach, what's wrong with your hair? Have you seen it? It's going all over the place!"

And that was the honest truth. When that prairie wind blew through Dallas, I have seen Jimmy's hair severely jacked up. If he was a black guy, Jimmy would never have that kind of problem. But since he isn't, I say Jimmy should have the right to put in his hair what he wants to.

So now I have said it, once and for all, and that is my final word on Jimmy Johnson's hair.

You gonna buy that?

I'm only joking and Jimmy knows it. But my rookie year in the league I'd never dare to, and it wasn't only because I still hadn't paid my dues. Jimmy Johnson, back then, was not the same person that everyone knows today. Though he'd already made his mark on college football, he hadn't won two straight Super Bowls. And here in the NFL, the biggest league there is, some people were still refusing to give him respect.

Many were openly critical of him, and that went double in Dallas. The season before, his own first year in the league, Jimmy's Cowboys had finished 1–15. Jimmy had also replaced Tom Landry, and some fans in Dallas hated him merely for that. I never thought this made any sense at all. Jerry Jones fired Tom Landry. Jimmy just accepted an open position. None of that seemed to matter in Dallas, though. My rookie year with the Cowboys, both the fans and the press were still at Jimmy's throat.

With that kind of pressure weighing on him, Jimmy in turn was extremely tough on us. Now, I don't mind some hardness in a head coach. At this level of competition, I think it's required. But I also like knowing my coach has some compassion. Today I know for a fact that Jimmy does. Back then, I couldn't see it. When I looked in Jimmy's eyes, I saw a man who felt besieged, a man obsessed with building a winning program, a man too wrapped up in himself to care about other people.

I'll never forget the first time he went off on me. It happened one Thursday at practice. Jimmy had us doing a drill on our two-minute offense, which we weren't executing smoothly during our games. As I ran a route to the left side of the field, Troy's pass came in low. Still, I thought I got my hands between the ground and the football. But Jimmy called it "no catch," and he was the referee.

Back in the huddle, Troy peered at the sideline to get the next play. He kept peering, and peering, until Jimmy screamed, "TIME OUT!" He was irked at David Shula, our offensive coordinator. It was David's job to get the play in on time.

Troy walked to the sideline, where he and David Shula could talk things out. Since we had a time-out anyway, I trotted over to Jimmy.

"Coach, I did catch that pass, you know," I said.

THE EMMITT ZONE

I was smiling, friendly, just wanting the man to know I made the play.

Jimmy said, "Get your butt in the huddle right now!"

I stared at him, surprised, and this time he screamed it. "GET YOUR BUTT IN THE HUDDLE RIGHT NOW!"

I just walked away from him, back to our huddle, but it bothered me all practice. I was upset that Jimmy had confronted me that way.

We didn't speak the following day, and I guess my irritation was on my face. One of Jimmy's assistant coaches came up to me and said, "What's up with you and Jimmy? Why are you frowning at him? He was just mad at somebody else yesterday. You caught him at a bad time."

"I didn't know I was frowning at him," I said. "But what he did yesterday was uncalled for. We had a time-out; I wasn't disrupting anything. And I have to be that cautious around my own coach?"

Jimmy and I didn't talk again the next day. The day after that he walked up to me before practice.

"Hey," Jimmy said, not giving me much.

"What's up, Coach?" I said, holding back too.

Jimmy said, "Oh, you still mad at me?"

We both smiled and the incident ended. But Jimmy stayed uptight the rest of that season. He was so quick to jump on people, even for something small, I think it was hard for some of our guys to play football. They were more concerned about Jimmy than their assignment.

But Jimmy has changed, in my opinion. Even though he still can't tolerate losing, he seems more relaxed about life in general now. I'm sure it had something to with all the winning we did, but I also think he was transformed by something else: the speech Jim Valvano made before he died.

It was March 4, 1993, about one month after we won our first Super Bowl, at ESPN's first annual ESPY awards. Jimmy and I were both in the crowd that night in New York. I won Performer of the Year in professional football. In all sports, amateur or pro, Jimmy was named the best manager/coach.

Jim Valvano, his body fighting its final bout with cancer, stood up and talked about never giving up. He also spoke about what is truly important—showing your love to those who mean the most to you, living every day with a sense of joy. Everyone there was crying, including me. And when Jimmy stood up to accept his award, he focused on the speech Coach Valvano just gave. He talked about how much it moved him and opened his eyes.

I didn't know if Jimmy was just being gracious, just saying what he felt he had to, so soon after Coach Valvano had talked. Then, in the months to come, Jimmy showed me that he meant what he said that evening. On a day-to-day basis, he seemed more at ease, more fun, more willing to express his real emotions. "I want you to know something, Emmitt," Jimmy told me one day out of the blue. "You're more than a good football player to me. There are guys in this league who are good, but they've never learned how to win. You're good and you're a winner."

I like to think so too, but it's nice hearing it from a man you've been through a lot with, and a man you never felt you could talk to at first.

We had another nice moment this last January, after we beat San Francisco to advance for the second straight year to the Super Bowl. As he and I were walking off the field together at Texas Stadium, Jimmy wrapped his arm around my neck. It was loud out there, and Jimmy shouted, "I love you!"

I shouted back, "I love you, too."

Jimmy yelled, "You mean a lot to me, you know!"

I yelled, "I know, Jimmy, I know!"

Sure, we'd just won a big game and we both felt sky-high. But in any circumstance, how many NFL coaches will tell their players they love them?

Since Jimmy doesn't show it often in public, most people never see this side of him. What they mostly see is his swagger, and his ego, and Lord knows the man has his share of both. One time a writer asked me, kidding around: "So who has a bigger ego, you or Jimmy Johnson?"

I laughed and told him, "At this level everybody has pride. You can't succeed in the NFL without it. But Jimmy's ego is bigger than mine. Much bigger than mine. WAY bigger than mine!"

That was the real deal. Only one guy on our team has an ego to rival Jimmy's. His name is Michael Irvin.

That's one way those guys differ from me, I guess. Like Jimmy and Michael, my dedication to winning is absolute, but they talk a lot more trash. On the other hand, both Michael and Jimmy are smart. Whenever they talked trash, I always felt their main purpose was throwing off our opponents. Or as Jimmy once said: "If I know there's already some seeds of doubt, I don't mind adding some fertilizer."

By the time Jimmy left Dallas, Michael was probably

the closest player to him. But Jimmy had good rapport with almost all our players, and I thought he had *great* rapport with our black guys. It's hard to say why exactly, since human nature is always tricky terrain, but it might've had something to do with Jimmy's blunt nature. He always told people just where they stood, not what he thought they wanted to hear. In an industry where most of the players are black, and management's mostly white, perhaps our black players responded to Jimmy's candor. I know that I did. I really don't care if my coach is politically correct. I just want a coach who will talk to me straight-out.

In relating to the black players on our team, Jimmy's background was also a possible factor. He grew up in Port Arthur, Texas, where he hung out and played ball with a number of black kids. As he said in his own book, *Turning the Thing Around,* he also worked with black people when he was a child. "After fourth grade," Jimmy said, "I got my first summer job, working for Daddy at the dairy. There were black and Mexican ladies working there. I rode a delivery truck as a route helper with a Cajun named Blackie. Ethnic interaction was so normal to me that I didn't actively think about it. Other than school hours, I associated with minorities all the time—afternoons, weekends, summers. And nothing negative was ever said or done."

When Jimmy got older and entered college coaching, he did his own part in ignoring racial barriers, recruiting many black athletes to play for him at Miami. But that wasn't just done from the kindness of his heart. Regardless of color, Jimmy wanted the best talent so he could keep winning.

■ ■ ■

Some coaches only look at the bottom line: Did we win this week or did we lose?

Not Jimmy Johnson. If we didn't play up to his standards—and up to our own—sometimes he blasted us after a victory.

It happened last season at Minnesota in a 37–20 win over the Vikings. Midway through the third quarter, we had a 27–6 lead, but then our defense allowed two touchdowns. Afterwards, in our locker room, Jimmy was already reaming the defense when Charles Haley walked in late. Charles had lingered outside an extra few minutes, mingling and shaking hands with some of the Vikings. The instant Charles came in Jimmy stopped shouting, but his face turned an even deeper shade of red.

Charles walked past him and Jimmy said, "No, Charles, you come stand up here with me."

"I'm fine right here," Charles said.

Jimmy said, "I want you up here with me."

Charles repeated, "I'm fine right here."

Charles can be just as stubborn as Jimmy, and if we stayed here all night, he didn't look as if he would move. So Jimmy finally said, "Hey! I don't want anyone else walking in late. Hurry up, do what you gotta do after the game, and get your butt in here!"

Then Jimmy finished his tirade, and guess what happened? The following Sunday, against the Jets, our defense caused four turnovers and nearly pitched a shutout, 28–7.

Jimmy's the first to admit he has a fiery temper, but he

EMMITT SMITH

also likes to preach the power of positive thinking, something he learned as a psychology major in college. In discussing his leadership style, Jimmy once said: "I never tell a running back, 'Don't fumble.' I never tell a placekicker, 'Don't miss.' I say to the running back, 'Protect the ball.' I say to the placekicker, 'Make this.' "

Well, Jimmy did *tend* to accentuate the positive. But the man was no Boy Scout. One time I heard him tell someone on our sideline, "You fumble that ball again I'm cutting your ass! I'm gonna put you back in the game now, but if you fumble again I'm cutting your ass tomorrow!" That's how Jimmy could get about fumbles and interceptions. He despised turnovers even more than penalties.

With that psych major of his, Jimmy also prided himself on his motivational skills, but I never felt that was the key to his success. Not that Jimmy was lacking in this regard. It's just that most NFL players drive themselves. They don't need coaches, or anyone else, to ignite them.

No, I think what Jimmy does best is recognize great athletes, and then make sure he doesn't stifle their talents. Jimmy behaved the same way with his assistant coaches. Before they left his staff for their own head coaching jobs, Jimmy hired Norv Turner and Dave Wannstedt, two of the sharpest coordinators in the league. Some head coaches might have felt threatened, kept them on a short leash. Jimmy did just the opposite. He gave them real authority— and everybody won. Norv and Dave helped Jimmy earn his two Super Bowl rings. Jimmy showcased their skills and now they run their own programs.

Besides his ability to hire great players and coaches—

and then let them breathe—Jimmy had this strange power I've never seen. He could predict, with amazing results, how our games would turn out. Jimmy told us one time before we played New Orleans: "Men, this will be a field position game. But we're gonna win it in the fourth quarter." That's almost exactly what happened. The final score was 17–13, Dallas.

A similar thing occurred before a game at Atlanta. Jimmy said, "This game scares me. If we play well, it's gonna be a dogfight, we may win by three points. But if we don't, we're gonna go down and get our butts blown out." Atlanta crushed us, 41–17.

I guess it was Jimmy's gut talking to him, and I guess that powerful gut was why he took so many gambles during big games. Fake punts, onside kicks, going for it on fourth down—those were Jimmy Johnson trademarks while he was at Dallas. And whether they worked or failed, I think the risks Jimmy took inspired our players. Nobody wants a coach who deals from fear.

In a season as long as the NFL's, nobody wants a coach with no sense of humor, either, and one thing Jimmy could do was make us laugh. One time he told us after practice: "You gotta remember, guys, when you go out there on that football field, and you ain't doing everything you can to improve yourself, you're cutting yourself. That's right. We never cut you. You cut yourself."

They never cut us? We cut ourselves? In a football player's eyes, that's called blowing some serious smoke. And even though Jimmy said it with a straight face, he quickly understood that we weren't buying it. When a few players started smiling, Jimmy did too.

EMMITT SMITH

Maybe it was his southwestern background, but Jimmy turned some of the funniest phrases in football. Last November we lost two games in five days, first to Atlanta on Sunday and then to Miami on Thanksgiving Day. At the time, both losses seemed huge, but Jimmy did not lose his cool. Looking at our record of 7–4, he felt we needed to win our final five games; otherwise we might not win the NFC East, and then if we made the playoffs we'd have to go in as a wild card.

At our first team meeting after Thanksgiving, Jimmy's basic message was, We just lost two in a row. Let's all come together right now and do whatever it takes. But this is how Jimmy said it: "Now listen to me, guys. We've got five weeks of tough football in front of us. Now I can hang from my **** for these five weeks, so we can get where we want to be. Can you guys go and hang from your **** for five weeks?"

It was silly. It broke the tension. And if you're a football fan you may already know how it ended: Including the playoffs, we won eight straight last year and wound up taking it all.

One time Jimmy cracked us up with a comment he made about Jerry. This was back in my rookie year, when their relationship still seemed pretty decent. Sometimes, on road trips, Jerry would let his various friends fly on our plane. Knowing that Jerry was planning on doing it this time, Jimmy called us together one day at practice.

"Coats and ties as usual," Jimmy said. "And I want you all to be on your best behavior. Jerry's got those damn yahoos flying with us on our plane!"

Jimmy looked surprised when everyone laughed; I

really don't think he was trying to be disrespectful. He just had this comical way of speaking his mind.

Sometimes, to keep us loose, he'd tell us about his own playing days in college. In 1964, the year his Arkansas team won the national championship, Jimmy started at nose guard. "Guys, you shoulda seen me," Jimmy would say. "I used to get in there and knock 'em out!" One time at practice he was in a great mood, racing around the field and wisecracking with people, when abruptly he stopped right in front of me. Dropping into his stance, Jimmy said, "Emmitt, I could take your head off! I could run right through ya!"

Then Jimmy was off and running before he could show me. That's because Coach knew the truth: He couldn't tackle me without a small army. I'd Earl Campbell his behind.

■ ■ ■

One afternoon at practice, I was sitting on the sideline on my helmet. Alvin Harper, our big-play receiver, was doing the same. Jimmy turned and saw us and he said, "Hey, Harper, you haven't made any Pro Bowl yet—get up off your helmet!" Alvin looked up, smiling, and got off his helmet. Just to rag on Alvin, I stayed there a second longer, and then I stood up too.

The point of the story is, yes, Jimmy did give some players a little more room than others. All coaches do it, but most of them won't admit it. Jimmy, being Jimmy, kept it out in the open for everybody to see. He'd even tell us about his scale, the one that started at one inch and ended at twelve. Some players fell near the one, some near the twelve, and most somewhere in the middle. If you had the nerve to ask, Jimmy would tell you precisely where he thought you had been playing.

One thing he didn't abide, from journeymen or stars, was letting the nightlife in Dallas interfere with our mission. Normally, Jimmy stayed out of our personal lives. But if he could tell the nightlife was killing someone, he'd call in that person to speak with him in private. Other times, without mentioning names, Jimmy would address us as a team.

"You guys know me by now," he'd say. "I'm not one to tell you to go home from here and only think about football, football, football. No, I'm not gonna do that; you're all grown men. But when you come here to this complex, you better come here prepared to *work*. If you're not prepared to work, and *your* nightlife is getting into *our* way, then I have a problem with you. So I'm telling you guys: Do not let the nightlife ruin your day job."

That ordinarily solved any problem. Though Jimmy was never a dictator, he was tough. And if any one of our players kept playing the fool, kept putting himself in front of our ball club, that player knew Jimmy would cut him and never look back. It all goes back to Jimmy's hunger for winning. Jimmy is more turned on by winning than anyone I've ever met. That's why everyone in this league wants to play for him. Nobody came here to lose.

I obviously don't see him as much as I did, but Jimmy and I are still friendly, and still connected by what we took part in together. I'm proud of Jimmy, too. He says just what he thinks and that alienates some people, but nobody can deny what he has accomplished. He won a national championship at Miami, and established them as a perennial contender. Then he helped resurrect the Cowboys, driving them from 1–15 to two straight Super Bowl wins. Jimmy had plenty of help from his players and coaching staff; he's always made sure to point that out himself. But as football coaches go, at any level, I think Jimmy Johnson is in a class by himself.

3
FAMILY
FIRST

From the way I used to thrash around inside her, my mom says she knew I was a boy. Once I was born, she knew that I would play football, just like my father. Because one day when I was a few months old, my mom did an experiment: She turned on a football game, then sat me a few feet in front of it in my swing. Even at such a young age, my mom says, my eyes would follow the motion. Then I'd watch even closer when something exciting happened.

My favorite team as a kid was the Dallas Cowboys. Growing up in Pensacola, Florida, the Falcons and Saints were closer, but a lot of the Cowboy games were also telecast. And they were the team I adopted. The players I liked most were Roger Staubach and Tony Dorsett. I admired Staubach for his scrambling, the comebacks he led, and his firm-but-quiet leadership. I admired Dorsett for all his exciting runs, and also his heart. Even though he wasn't big, he always seemed willing to run inside.

I can still remember one Sunday afternoon when I was four or five. Lying down on the floor with my father and cousins, watching the Dallas game on TV, I announced to the room, "One day I'm gonna play for the Dallas Cowboys." It was just a nice dream. Nobody had an inkling it would come true.

I started organized football when I was eight. Even before that, I played sandlot games with my younger brother Erik and my older cousins. After diving around in the mud and grass, we'd come back to my house filthy and anger my mom. So we started doing what we considered ingenious. Once we left the house, we turned our pants and shirts inside out before we played football. Then we turned them back around before we went home. Like our mom couldn't tell when she did the laundry?

Once I turned eleven or twelve, I did get into my share of mischief, but I was never really a troubled child. I always had good self-esteem, always had lots of friends and good times, playing pinball machines and collecting bottles, fishing and hunting with BB guns, taking fifteen-mile bike rides all over Pensacola. In retrospect, those long rides were probably great for my stamina and my legs. But I was just a kid then, having a ball. It was all about fun, not training.

EMMITT SMITH

Eventually there were seven of us in our family: my mother, Mary; my father, Emmitt, Jr.; my older sister, Marsha; myself; and my younger brothers Erik, Emory, and Emil. With five children to clothe and feed, we never had much extra money, but that never seemed like anything we couldn't handle. Much more important to me than how much money we had, I lived with both my parents, and I knew that I was wanted. From not only my parents but my whole family, I learned how to love, how to behave, how to give respect and earn it. Nothing in life, including pro football, means as much to me as they do. My career could end tomorrow if I got badly injured. My family will always be there.

We've all been there for each other as long as I can recall, but sometimes life wasn't easy. My father drove a city bus, and that was our only income. Mom didn't get a paid job until later on, preferring to stay at home and work on raising her kids. Until I was eight years old, we rented a house in a government housing project. At some meals, we ate government cheese and powdered milk.

There were worse projects around, but ours had its dangers. We heard shootings at night. My father had belongings stolen from him. Outside, between the small houses, rats as big as raccoons scuttled around. And I had fights in the 'hood that started when I got jumped.

I saw drugs in the projects, too, but never even experimented with them. Drugs were always a turnoff when I was growing up. Especially after what happened with me and my buddy Robert one afternoon. Walking to football practice, we saw a car pull up with a white gentleman in-

THE EMMITT ZONE

side. From the way he gestured to us, I thought the guy was lost and needed directions. I walked toward his car but couldn't quite hear what he said, so I kept coming closer, with Robert a few feet behind me.

The guy said, "Kid, can you shoot me up?"

Not knowing what he meant, I just said, "What?"

He said it again. "Shoot me up."

Then he showed me his needle.

I stared at it a moment and then I looked at him. Inside his eyes I saw some kind of craziness.

Before I could even turn, Robert took off running and left me alone. After I beat it out of there too, I never forgot that man's eyes or his dirty-looking needle. Unlike a lot of children, I never even felt curious about drugs.

Still, I was just a kid; it wasn't like I formed my values alone. I blew off drugs for the same reason I never ran with a truly bad crowd: If I got in serious trouble, my parents would tear my ass up. Love and discipline, discipline and love. In our family it always seemed to be part of one whole.

■　■　■

In many American homes, it's the mother who feels anxious about her son playing football and the father who nudges him toward it. We were the exception to the rule. My mom never missed one of my games. My father at first didn't want me to play football.

Even though he never said it flat out, that was the vibe I got. I never asked him why he felt that way either, mostly because he never forbid me from playing. But also because, like a lot of young boys, I was a little scared of my father back then.

My mother did most of the whipping, but my father always had this real powerful presence. Unless he had something significant to say, he didn't talk much. His facial expression was often intense, from the anger he carried within. I don't know exactly where his anger came from, but I do know times got hard for him financially. There were holidays, I'm sure, when my father wished he could bring us more gifts. But the great thing about my dad was, I never heard him complain. Not about money, not about anything. And while I'm not even close to being that tough, I do think my father gave me some of his inner strength.

As for his anger, he mostly kept it inside. Unless, that is, I failed to do my share of the household chores. If I shirked that, I knew my father might blow, so I never took any chances. When I was a kid I washed dishes, cleaned bathrooms, vacuumed, dusted, made beds, hung wet clothes on the line, raked the yard, and cut the grass. Then, when I was twelve, I got my first real job, at the Magnolia Nursing Home, where my mother worked in the office. I did landscaping and janitorial work, and sometimes I pushed around elderly folks in their wheelchairs. I really enjoyed that job, because older people know so much about life.

I also liked having money to buy my own clothes. Up until then, Mom and I had been going at it about my wardrobe. About to start high school, I wanted some clothes that were more up-to-date; she wanted to keep buying clothes she could afford.

THE EMMITT ZONE

Getting the nursing home job and having some cash in my pocket didn't suddenly make me the best-dressed kid in my class. But at least I was closing the gap.

■ ■ ■

Back in the early 1960s, my father played running back and defensive back at Washington High in Pensacola. He rarely discusses that time in his life, but other folks in Pensacola do. "Son, your daddy was something else in high school," they say. My dad then received some college scholarship offers, but with two bad knees that frequently needed draining, he went straight to work when he left high school.

He never stopped appreciating the game, though. And by the time I was nine or ten, he had put aside his reservations about my playing football. Later on, my first two years of high school, my father took the game back up himself. Bad knees and all, he played semipro ball for the Pensacola Wings.

It was pretty cool. All during the week, my dad drove his bus and we went to school. But our weekends revolved around football. I'd play my high school games on Friday nights. Saturday mornings, we'd watch my brother Emory play youth-league ball. Saturday nights, we'd check out my dad playing wide receiver and safety. I'm not lying: Forty years old and the man could still play.

My mom was in the stands those evenings too. I might be a little biased, but she's the most supportive person I've ever met. As gentle and soft and caring as she could be, though, she also accepted no nonsense. If we ever tried playing ball before we finished our homework, she'd get on our case before we could reach the door. There wasn't any negotiating, either. No schoolwork, no athletics. No excuses.

One night I learned what would happen if I disobeyed her. We didn't have HBO when I was a kid, so I went to a friend's house to watch a movie. When it started getting good, I called my mother and told her I would be late.

"No, you come home right now," she said.

"But, Mom, we're in the middle of a good movie."

"You can see the end of it some other time. Now it's getting late and I want you home."

I hung up the phone and watched the end of the movie. Where was the harm in that?

It was upside my head when I walked in our front door.

I came in after nine. Mama had just woken up and wasn't feeling too well. Pop! She smacked me in the head with an open palm.

I was embarrassed and upset, but I deserved it. My parents only had a few major rules: Never break the law. Hit the books hard and hit them before sports. Be on time when you tell someone you will, and always be home before dark. It wasn't that much to ask, and I ended up telling my mother I was sorry. She said she felt bad too, but she did it in her own way.

She told me, laughing, "You're getting too big for me to whip you with switches. That's why I gotta start beating you with my hands." She was just playing, but her message sunk in. Her children would never feel alone or neglected. At the same time, her children would understand limits.

THE EMMITT ZONE

With my father working long hours, in the Smith family it was always Mom, Mom, Mom. When I turned eight and first played organized football, she was the one who took me to get signed up. In those days I played quarterback, but I wasn't exactly the classic pocket passer. If my receivers were covered, I scampered right out of there.

I played that year for the Salvation Army. I'll never forget our final game, against our number one nemesis, Brent Ballpark. In youth-league ball, as we moved from level to level, we couldn't exceed a particular weight. So I had to climb on the scale like everyone else, except I was already a very large child. The morning before we played Brent Ballpark, I made the weight with my uniform on, but the Brent coach wasn't satisfied with that. He wanted me to strip down and get on the scale again. When I still made the weight, undressed, the Brent coach looked around and said arrogantly, "It doesn't matter. We're gonna whip 'em anyway."

Already hot that I'd been put through this, my coach said, "Oh yeah? We're gonna kick your butt!"

After the weigh-in, my coach pulled me aside so we could talk in private. He said, "Emmitt, I'm gonna make you a deal. If we beat these guys, I'll take you anywhere you wanna eat."

We romped all over Brent that afternoon; we ate their lunch. That night my coach took me out for a modest dinner.

It wasn't just that one game. The entire time that I played childhood football, my size and weight was an ongoing issue. I guess I've come full circle: Now that I play

EMMITT SMITH

running back in the NFL, some people call me small at 5-9$\frac{1}{2}$ and 209 pounds. I don't feel small with a football in my hands. I feel lethal. But up until I started winning those rushing titles, I still heard people questioning my size. I heard it questioned when I was a child too. Only then everyone said I was too big.

Having a larger body, at times I felt like people were staring at me. Before some of my games, my mom had to bring my birth certificate with her. Otherwise other parents and coaches thought I was an older boy brought in to play as a ringer. By the time I turned eleven, I usually had to lose weight if I wanted to play in leagues with my own age group. Lose weight? I was growing, man! Growing and hungry, and most of my weight was muscle. Where exactly was I supposed to lose it? No matter how many miles I ran, sometimes I just couldn't.

So from age eleven on, I mostly played football with older kids. It wasn't the end of the world. And I'm sure that it elevated my game. But there were times I really wished I were smaller, so I could play with kids from my own grade. Because even back then, I didn't want people looking at me as an object. I wanted to be seen as a person first, and only then as an athlete.

■　■　■

Besides getting my first taste of organized football, the year I turned eight included another milestone. Our family moved out of the housing project we lived in.

Though my day-to-day environment improved, I never felt like I was escaping. It wasn't as if we were migrating to the suburbs. We only moved four blocks away, so anytime I felt like shooting hoops, or just checking out my friends, I could trot to the projects in two or three minutes. In a sense, then, I never left.

Our new house was on North G Street. It sat in the roomy backyard behind our grandparents' house. Though it was larger than the small place we had in the projects, I still shared a bedroom with two of my brothers. Since our room only had two beds, most nights I crashed downstairs on the sofa. I wasn't being a martyr—I had more privacy there.

For me, the best thing about our new home was living that much closer to my father's parents. They enjoyed it too. My dad was their only child, so this gave them a chance to fill up their life with more children.

Just like my own father, my grandpa was quiet, hard-working, and tough. For forty years, he did heavy manual labor at the Armstrong Industries plant in Pensacola. When he finally retired, he could not recall missing a single day of work.

Before he did retire, my grandfather did shift work: 9 to 5, 3 to 11, 11 to 7. So even before we moved in right behind them, I spent some nights at their house. That way I could help my grandmother, Erma Lee. She was a paraplegic, and my dad and I would go there when Grandpa had to work night shifts. My dad would lift his mom out of her wheelchair and lay her down in her bed. Then he'd go back to the projects and I'd stay there with my grandma. Whatever she needed, I'd get it for her during the night. Or else I'd turn her over on her other side, so she could sleep more comfortably.

EMMITT SMITH

My grandmother recently died, and I loved that woman so much. Although her body was weak, she was the strongest person I knew emotionally. My grandma endured with optimism and grace. Her smile lit every room. She was a praying woman, too, a spiritual woman always reading the Bible.

Growing up Baptist in the Deep South, we all spent time in prayer. Today, I am more aware of the place in my life the Lord has. As a child, I mostly liked going to church because of the music. But even then, once the clapping and singing ended, my brothers and I had a hard time sitting still. So Mama would pinch our arms for talking too much, or lift us back up by our ears when we slouched too low. Then, if we sat calmly in the pews, later that day she'd let us go play football.

4
A RUNNER
IS BORN

I was nine years old when football threw me for my first loss.

I had just graduated from Mini-Mites to Mites, the league for boys nine and ten, when my new coach, Mr. Warren, told me just minutes before our first practice: "You're not playing quarterback this year, son."

I said, "What?"

He said, "I'm gonna line you up in the back of the I. We're gonna toss you the football and let you run."

I didn't fuss or make a scene. I didn't question Mr. Warren. But I was nine years old and my spirits sagged. In order to be my team's most valuable player, I thought I had to play quarterback.

Pretty quickly I saw it wasn't true. Our very first week of practice, I felt natural running the ball from the back of the I. As a former quarterback known more for his running than passing, I was already shifty and strong. Now that I was lining up several yards deeper, I picked up another advantage: My vision improved. Except for the wide receivers and cornerbacks, I could see every player on either team. I could see changes in coverage from play to play. Just before the ball was snapped, I could look at a defense and know where the hole would be, regardless of what hole that play had been designed for.

At first, I thought this happened only because I was lining up deeper. After watching some other runners, I realized my vision was something special I had. Today, as a pro, I think it's still one of my strengths. I can see things on a football field that other runners don't.

My first season at tailback, I also liked the physical side of my new position. I liked the idea of being a tough guy— a guy who takes a lot of hits, but also administers them. In less than a week or so, I didn't care if I ever played quarterback again. And once I put my whole heart into it, that's when my career as a running back took off.

Look at the opportunities, not the negatives. This was one lesson I learned from playing sports. I learned another the year I turned ten, when the Salvation Army closed down its football program. My brothers and I were suddenly free agents, just some football-playing fools looking for action. We signed up with Bellview, a youth-league team widely known for its hard-nosed tradition. Our first day of practice, my new coaches let me play linebacker. I *loved* playing linebacker, and I racked some people up. I broke one kid's finger and fractured another kid's tailbone. Nobody wanted anyone to get hurt, but football is football and my new coaches were wide-eyed. Who is this kid?

Though I was only ten, the very next day they promoted me to Midgets, where I played with kids eleven and twelve. First Midget-league practice, after just racking two kids the day before, I got racked myself. I was running the ball in a tackling drill. A kid named Billy Sprague hit me so hard, I had a headache all day and night. Lesson number two: You may be bad, but other guys are too. So keep your pride but never lose your humility.

With some of my teammates two years older than me, I didn't even start on offense that year. I was more of a third-down back, or a trick-play back. I was out there scoring touchdowns on wing reverses, cutting back and reversing my field, all that kind of flashy stuff. I also ran back kicks and punts and started on defense at linebacker. Doing all those different things on a football field, I had a blast. It was my favorite year of my childhood football career.

On May 15, 1980, I turned eleven. That football season, I had to monitor my weight if I wanted to stay in Midgets. So on Friday nights before Saturday games, my coach had me sleep at his home, where he could keep an eye on what I was eating. His name was Charlie Edgar. His son Jody played quarterback for us. Coach Edgar didn't starve me, but he fed me low-fat foods. Then, on Saturday morning, I'd wake up early and run off those last few pounds.

Looking back on it, those Friday nights were important. The Edgar family was white, and even though I'd competed against some white kids, I'd never slept in a white person's home. It was a great education—a positive one. Watching the Edgars, I saw that white families were close-knit too. I realized the Edgars were beautiful people, who embraced me like I was one of their own. Even when the football season ended, I still played with all the Edgar boys, climbing trees and running through woods, just being out in nature. The decency and kindness the Edgars gave me, at age eleven, is one reason I've never felt prejudiced toward white folks. Plus I've always understood, instinctively, that all people deserve to be judged one by one.

Strange as it may sound, I never encountered racism until I got older and left for college. My parents never mentioned it much either. They talked about black history and black pride, but they never railed against white people. As for the city of Pensacola, I'm certain there were racists living there—not because it's the South, but because there are racists all over the globe. Nobody ever put their racism on me, though. And I can look back right now and see football fields I played on in Pensacola, fields with black kids and white kids running around together, wrestling with each other, helping each other up after a hit. I can still see it, because that's the way it was.

■ ■ ■

Just because I avoided serious trouble, it doesn't mean I never raised any hell. When I tell my mom about certain things I did, she looks like she wants to whip me just for old times' sake.

When I was eleven, a few neighborhood guys and I

EMMITT SMITH

used to place a log in the street. Since it was a large log, we'd wait until sunset, when it was harder for motorists to see. Then we'd hide in the bushes, laughing like crazy each time a car lost its muffler. Sometimes we'd fire rocks at the passing cars, too. One night we pelted a car with rocks at the same time it hit the log. Then somebody said, "Oh, man, that's a police car!"

We took off like Ronnie Lott was chasing us. But even though we didn't get caught, I knew, deep in my heart, that I never should have been doing this kind of mischief. And after that episode I pretty much stopped.

Okay, okay, I did mess up a little this one other time. Late one summer afternoon, three buddies and I got dropped off by an older friend at a movie theater ten miles from our own neighborhood. By the time the movie ended, it was almost eight and getting dark. But our older friend wasn't anywhere to be found. With all our money spent on tickets and candy, how were we supposed to get back home?

Already running late, we knew we'd be grounded for sure if we walked the ten miles home. So we called a taxi to pick us up. We gave the cabbie a bogus address, a few blocks from our real houses. To our amazement, he stopped at an old, abandoned building. We all looked at each other, thinking, We're finished.

Somehow, the guy didn't seem to notice. So we told him we'd run inside and get the cash from our mom. The empty house was so dark, we were bouncing off walls and giggling, tripping all over each other and acting like jokers. When we finally climbed out a window and scaled a fence,

THE EMMITT ZONE

we thought we were real clever. But we were just being jerks. The guy was making his living and we stiffed him.

Fortunately, I had enough common sense to not get much dumber than that. As a result, I never got hooked up with the true delinquents. In fact, my biggest childhood trauma was not such a trauma at all: For one entire season I couldn't play football.

I attended Brownsville Middle School at the time. Since it had no football program, my only choice was still playing youth league. That wasn't the problem; my weight was. At age thirteen I already weighed 180, and league rules put the ceiling at 160. I never even thought about shedding those twenty pounds. I was still muscular, not fat.

Thinking I would go crazy not playing football, at first I got depressed. Then Coach Edgar came through for me again. To make sure I still felt wanted and involved, he let me coach the running backs that year. It could have been weird, a thirteen-year-old coaching his own teammates, but the guys were totally cool. In retrospect, the experience was a good one. I learned I could survive without playing football.

On the other hand, I also knew high school football was only a year away, which meant I had something exciting to contemplate. As for staying in shape until then, Brownsville did have track and basketball teams, and I was a member of both. Track was fine, but basketball was my passion. And don't think for a second I couldn't go to the hoop. Playing point guard or center, depending on where I was needed, I had a decent jumper and I could almost dunk. But I was no prima donna—I also pulled boards and played tenacious defense.

EMMITT SMITH

The season before, in seventh grade, I had helped Brownsville win the city championship. Even though we didn't repeat, we had another good run in eighth grade. When our season ended, my coach considered me one of the city's top prospects. Looking ahead to high school, I had every intention of still playing basketball.

■ ■ ■

Every so often, if an athlete is lucky, he meets an older man who makes him a better young man. I met that person the spring of my eighth grade. His name was Dwight Thomas, and he was the new football coach at Escambia High, where my middle school had a track meet one afternoon. During a break from his team's spring football practice, he walked over and we introduced ourselves.

"Would you like to play football next year at Escambia High?" Coach Thomas asked.

"Yes, sir," I said without hesitation. Some of his players were teammates of mine in youth league. And my family lived in the Escambia district anyway.

He asked me what position I wanted to play. Tell you the truth, I wanted desperately to play both ways in high school—like I said, I loved playing defense. But I already knew Coach Thomas didn't allow it. With him, it was one or the other. That way more kids could play.

"Where do I have the best chance of starting?" I said.

"Offense," he said.

In that case, I told him, I'd like to play running back.

5
FOR THE
JOY OF IT

've heard about high school football in Texas and California, and I know those states produce some dynamite athletes. But Florida high school football may just be the best in the country. To name only a few, here's some guys besides me who played at Florida high schools and later the NFL: Bob Hayes, Ted Hendricks, Jack Youngblood, Deacon Jones, Larry Little, Rickey Jackson, Wilber Marshall, Sammy Smith, Louis Oliver, Anthony Carter, Lorenzo White, Michael Irvin, Bennie and Brian Blades, Wes Chandler, and Deion Sanders.

Unreal, huh?

So how can one state turn out so much high-powered talent?

Some people say it's the sunshine, allowing Florida kids to play football year-round. Other people say it's the first-rate youth leagues, like the ones that I played in. I've also heard it's the sandy, pliant soil, how excellent it is for building up young legs.

All that's probably true. But I think the biggest single reason is Florida's spring practice—one month of off-season drills, topped off at the end by a "spring jamboree." That's where several local high schools would get together for a rotating scrimmage with actual game conditions. Spring jamborees were so intense, college recruiters would flock to them from all over. So they not only helped the players get ready for fall, they also helped them get noticed.

As for my own high school team, its football program was terrible when I came there. In the previous eighteen years, Escambia High had only had one winning season. In the last three years its record was 3–27, including 1–9 the season before I arrived.

Those numbers didn't thrill me. They didn't freak me out, either. For one thing, I love a challenge. For another, I knew in Coach Thomas we had a strong leader. He never talked down to his players. He never embarrassed us when we made mistakes. He also never let us cut even one corner. That's an important line for a coach to be able to walk—at any level of football.

Coach Thomas also took over the job at a perfect time for his players. He had just been fired elsewhere and felt he had something to prove. After four winning years at a larger Florida high school, after posting a record of 30–12, he was called into the principal's office one day. The principal told him: "We really need to win a state championship this season. In order to do it, we need a coach who has already won one."

"He wanted my resignation by four-thirty," Coach Thomas has said. "He got it at four twenty-nine. I told him I was going to find the worst team in the state and come back and kick his ass."

Escambia wasn't *that* bad, but here's what I find unique about Dwight Thomas: He gets fired from a job for a horrible reason. He vows to get even. He takes a job at a high school known for its losing. And when I showed up for our first day of practice that fall, I learned that he had just cut twenty-six seniors! They weren't attending class, so he wouldn't let them play football. He didn't stop at that point, either. By the end of my freshman year, we only had four or five seniors on our entire squad.

Talk about sending a message.

Coach Thomas told us he had only three rules: Be where you're supposed to be; be there when you're supposed to be there; and be doing there what you're supposed to be doing. If we broke these rules, he told us, he wouldn't make us run laps or hold us out of a game. We would be gone, that day.

I got those rules loud and clear. Back at Brownsville Middle School, I'd gotten paddled a couple times for showing up late to class. In four years at Escambia High, I was never late for school or football practice.

THE EMMITT ZONE

With all those seniors cut from our team, we had no choice but to go with youth. Along with ten or eleven sophomores, another freshman and I started that year.

In my first high school game, I gained 115 yards and scored 2 touchdowns. Later that season, I went for 205 and 210 yards. It was exciting for me to play this well as a freshman, but it came as no surprise. God and my parents gave me a natural talent. All I had to do was apply myself. And up until then, that combination was working pretty well. I'd been gaining a lot of yards since the peewee leagues.

Even though we were young, I was also surrounded by excellent athletes. In the course of my career at Escambia High, I played with Sam Bettis, the starting tailback before I arrived, and a guy who remade himself into a punishing fullback. At wide receiver we had my friend Marzette Porterfield, one of the fastest sprinters in the state. At defensive line we had Lamar "Chili Dog" Williams, who bench-pressed 400 pounds. We had defensive backs Walter David and Sean Culliver, smart and fast enough to play man-to-man, but rough enough to stop the run. We also had Pat Moore, a linebacker who could stop trucks if they came through his turf.

And guiding and shaping us all, we had Coach Thomas. A natural leader, he put together a team that loved one another. When teams are winning, you hear the word "love" thrown around a lot. I mean it literally. We played for each other in high school. Not for money, not for glory, but for each other. If that sounds corny, so be it; that's the way I felt about my high school teammates.

EMMITT SMITH

I attribute a lot of that to Coach Thomas. He taught us to look beyond ourselves, which isn't always easy for adolescents to do. As he once said, "How we raise these kids affects how they'll raise their kids. They need to be taught some discipline and character. Christ strove to teach these qualities, and when His people got them, He stepped back and watched them work. That's what coaches do. We step back on Friday night and watch them work."

■ ■ ■

It wasn't all positive notes my freshman year. Playing our crosstown rival, Pensacola High, we got humiliated, 51–0. In another game, against Milton High, we were running an option play. Our quarterback faked up the middle to our fullback, then began running east and west behind the line of scrimmage. I was running behind him, trailing the option. As our quarterback kept the ball and turned the corner, I looked upfield to follow the play—and a guy flew out of nowhere and nearly broke my jaw. Then he stood over me, talking trash, like he really accomplished something. It turned out my jaw wasn't broken, but it was sore and tender the rest of the season. Excuse my French, but if I saw that guy today I'd probably whip his butt. That shot wasn't just cheap, it was illegal.

Still, what a year for Escambia High. After going 1–9 the season before, our team went 7–3. We wanted more, much more, but we all felt proud of what we accomplished. Escambia wasn't a laughingstock anymore. We were a dangerous team on the rise.

After football I moved right into basketball season. I

thought I'd dominate the floor, just as I had in seventh and eighth grade. Instead I developed a sudden confidence problem: I couldn't deal with throwing up bricks.

As a freshman football player, I had just started pumping iron seriously. In the process I managed to screw up my jump shot. Meanwhile, I was now playing hoops at the high school level, against guys who were working at it all year long. They were on another plane, and I couldn't handle it mentally. So even though I made varsity as a freshman, I quit the basketball team. I gave it another shot my sophomore year, and it happened again: I got eaten up and I left the team. From that point on I played only high school football. As much as I loved playing basketball, sometimes I still regret quitting like that. I guess that's all part of growing up, though. You learn to be less impatient and more determined.

■ ■ ■

Spring football. My second year at Escambia. It was 1985 and I was just turning sixteen.

One day before spring practice, I was sitting next to our fullback, Sam Bettis, while he sorted through five or six letters.

"What are those?" I said.

"Letters from colleges," he said.

"What? How come I don't get those?"

Already a junior, Sam said, "Don't worry about it. Your day will come. You're gonna have so many of them, you'll get sick of looking at them."

Sam would talk to me that spring about different colleges—who had quality teams and quality coaches, and also who he was planning on staying away from. It was mostly football talk. Then one afternoon he said, "It's not just about athletics, you know. If I'm good enough in high school, I can get a *scholarship* to college. They'll pay for my education, I can play college football at the same time, and perhaps someday go into professional ball."

That's when it struck me: If I keep performing in class and on the field, I'll have the same opportunity Sam does. I thought that was fantastic. Here I was, sixteen years old, and I had some rough idea of my future. It might not ever pan out—I was only a sophomore. But it was clearly something worth striving for.

A few months later, the summer before my sophomore season, my first college letter arrived. It came from the University of Florida. It was just a preliminary letter. By changing a couple items here and there, they probably sent the same letter to thousands of high school players. But I couldn't wait to get home and show my family. After only one year of high school ball, one major college already knew who I was.

■   ■   ■

Even once I got to the NFL, my father told a reporter, "It's funny, in a way. Watching him run today is the same as it was then. The only difference is that, when he was eight, he would run off and leave his blocking. At nine, he learned to follow it."

Well, my running style changed again my sophomore year. As a raw, pumped-up freshman, I mostly ran over people. My sophomore year I refined my game. I still ran through people when I had to, but I was also shaking them with moves, or simply sprinting right by them.

One game I'll never forget came against Rickards High. Though both my ankles were sprained, I wanted to play. Then I tested them in warm-ups, and they felt swollen and shaky, so our coaches decided to leave me on the sideline. Gerald Williams played great in the first half as my replacement, but Rickards had a good squad and took the lead. Late in the fourth quarter, with our team losing by 7, I finally got in there. On our 89-yard TD drive to tie the game, I gained about 85 yards and I was the hero. Then something horrible happened in overtime. On a running play near their goal line, I fumbled into their end zone and they recovered.

I felt punched in the belly.

I felt like a dog.

I felt I'd cost us the game.

Then, just as swiftly, the game swung back in our direction. Rickards could not move the ball and our offense came back out. Our field goal kicker won it for us in overtime.

Nevertheless, I'll always remember how weird I felt that night. Elated that we won, I was also relieved that I wasn't the goat. But I couldn't forgive myself for fumbling in overtime. I could barely look at my coaches and teammates. Amateur or professional, fumbling has to be the lowest feeling in football.

One day at practice my sophomore year, I must have fumbled four or five times. I don't know where my head was at. Neither did Jimmy Nichols, our offensive coordinator. His son Johnny played quarterback for us. Johnny was already one of my dearest friends. Later on, I'd be best man at his wedding. But that didn't stop his father from jumping in my face now.

"Son, this isn't youth-league ball anymore," Coach Nichols said. "You will not be a running back for this team if you keep fumbling the ball. You won't be a great running back anywhere—not here, not in college, not in the NFL—if you keep FUMBLING THE FOOTBALL!"

I was so ticked off at him and at myself, I pulverized one of our players the next time I carried the ball. Probably hurt the kid.

But Coach Nichols made me a better tailback that year. Because from that day forward, he had me doing fumbling drills left and right. Recover the football, recover the football, recover the football. Diving around on the ground, scraping my elbows and knees, I got Coach Nichols's message: You won't have to recover the ball if you don't drop it.

Ever since then, when I was sixteen, I started taking pride in not laying down the football. In four years of high school, I carried the ball about 1,100 times, and only had 5 or 6 fumbles.

My sophomore year at Escambia High was an unbelievable one. With a 12–2 record, first we made the state playoffs. Then we won the whole darn thing. Few people would've believed it a few years before, but Escambia High was the class 3-A state champ.

In the championship game we defeated Bartow, a high school in central Florida. They had to play us on our home field, but it still seemed to me like they had the edge. Bartow, without exception, was the scariest high school team I'd ever seen. I was 5-9½. Their entire team averaged over 6 feet tall; they had some guys that went all the way to 6-6. They weren't just tall, either. Those boys were ripped. Some of them even had beards! To me, they looked like guys in the NFL. And as I was standing around before the game, I said to one of my teammates, "Oh my God, we're in trouble now! These are some big old jokers!" I was kidding, but I wasn't.

Preparing myself to get hit, and hit, and hit, I ran on the field feeling utterly intense. I guess my teammates were just as jacked-up: We drove down the field our first possession, Bartow High couldn't do a thing with our running game, and suddenly all our nervousness was gone. Now we were intimidating them.

That's why I love a powerful running game: It not only moves the chains, it can also take a psychological toll. Because when you're pounding the ball down the other team's throat, there's nothing fancy about it. It's just straight-out, physical football. But defensive players like thinking that *they're* the physical ones. So once you prove you can manhandle them on the ground, they may start doubting themselves. If they do, it's only a matter of time.

Against Bartow High, they were so demoralized by our running game—and so far behind on the scoreboard—I felt we had the state championship won by halftime. We came into our locker room feeling fantastic, the little guys whipping the giants. Then, to our amazement, we realized our head coach was irate.

EMMITT SMITH

"They have no respect for us," Coach Thomas started screaming. "They're lying down out there. This is our football field, and we want a *game!* Now when you go back out, you better not respect them! They don't respect us enough to even give us a game!"

We blasted out of that locker room in a frenzy. Our locker room itself was up on a hill, with our stadium down below it, in a bowl. Our starting quarterback got so hyped up, he tripped and fell all the way down the entire hill. One of the funniest things I've ever seen.

■ ■ ■

By my junior year, I was probably the most feared runner in our district. And certain schools were clearly gunning for me.

Inside the stadium at Pensacola High, we'd see signs reading R.I.P EMMITT SMITH, or R.I.P 24. I got a kick out of it, and all it did was fire me up even more.

In one of the biggest games in the history of our city, we opened our junior year against Pensacola Woodham. It's rare for a first game to be this important, but Woodham was more than our heated rival; both our teams were also defending state champs. While we'd won 3-A the season before, Woodham had won 4-A. This year, Escambia High had also moved up to 4-A. With an influx of students, we were now among the largest schools in the state. So naturally this game got hyped like crazy. In Florida, the 4-A champ is considered the king of the state. Here were two local rivals who figured to be in the running, and also two high school teams ranked nationally.

THE EMMITT ZONE

We played them at Woodham Stadium, to a packed crowd of mixed loyalties. With two minutes left in the game, our team behind by a point but our offense on the move, I took a helmet to a hip that I'd already hurt. I didn't want to come off, but I could barely walk. When our drive stalled, all the pressure fell on our kicker, Alan Ward. Alan nailed it from 50 yards! And we knocked out Woodham High in the showdown in Pensacola.

The rest of my junior year, I played my finest high school football to date. We were now playing 4-A, against stronger competition, and that season I rushed for seven 200-yard games. In the second-biggest statistical day of my life, I also went off against Milton High. I carried 28 times for 301 yards, and on one touchdown run I broke about seven tackles. By the way, remember Milton High? They were that team from my freshman year, the one with the cheap-shot artist who almost broke my jaw. In my four years against Milton, I gained 855 yards. Not that I held a grudge.

With the kind of squad we had my junior year, we often blew people out. So once a game was in hand, Coach Thomas would pull our starters and let the second team play. I never told him this, but I always wanted him to leave me out there. According to what I'd heard, some runner in Tallahassee had once gained 400 yards in a high school game. I wanted that record badly, and a few games I felt I had a decent shot. Then we'd start killing a team and I'd find myself on the bench. I know that sounds greedy, but you have to be on your way to a monstrous game—and then get yanked—to totally understand it. Besides, most good running backs *are* a little bit greedy. We see those yards out there and we want to gobble them up.

After going 13–1 my junior year, this time we played for the 4-A championship. Rather than do it on our own field, as we had the season before, we had to try winning it 400 miles from home.

The night before the big game, we stayed in a hotel in Lakeland, Florida, about thirty minutes northeast of Tampa. When a few teammates and I turned on the TV in our room, we saw an interview with our opponents from Bradenton Southeast. Even before this, all we'd been hearing about was Bradenton's awesome defense. Ranked first in the state of Florida, its stats were out of this world. No offense had ever done this against Bradenton Southeast, no offense had ever done that.

Now they were talking trash on local TV. With the news cameras rolling, they were actually hitting their tackling dummies, then saying, "This is what we'll do tomorrow to Emmitt Smith!" They kept talking noise, until we were ready to play them right there in our hotel room. At one point I said to our TV set, "Yeah, but those tackling dummies you're hitting don't hit back!"

About noon the following day, we drove the thirty minutes to Bradenton Southeast High. As part of our custom for road games, we wanted to walk around on the other team's field, to familiarize ourselves and check its playing condition. Since it was only noon, most of the Bradenton students were on their lunch break. The moment they saw our bus, it seemed like the whole student body came charging at us.

That's when it got funny. Since this was a road game, Coach Thomas had us all wearing our usual outfits—blue slacks, white shirts, blue ties. Only this time, we also wore sombreros. On our way to the championship game, we'd been traveling up and down the entire state. At one of the tourist stops we all bought sombreros.

So we're sitting in our bus wearing huge Mexican hats, and the Bradenton student body is woofing itself hoarse. Even some of their football players were out there, screaming that we were punks and all the rest. Before we stepped outside, Coach Thomas gave us an order: Don't say one word. Don't even crack a smile.

That's what we did. We just took our big hats and checked out the field, marched back onto our bus, and returned to our hotel. We slept that afternoon, ate our pregame meal, then came back to take care of business.

Bradenton scored the first time they got the ball. Their stadium erupted, as if they would stomp these panhandle fools.

That was pretty much the end of their night.

Every outrageous defensive statistic they had, we trampled. We won by three touchdowns, I had about 160 yards rushing, and their guys were moaning and groaning by the fourth quarter, due to the whipping we gave them on *their* home field.

They had it coming. Unless you can back it up, you don't talk trash to the Escambia Gators.

And that was how we won our second state championship.

EMMITT SMITH

■   ■   ■

As we did throughout our childhoods, my brother Erik and I had some conflicts my senior year. To fully understand why—besides the simple fact that we were siblings—you have to understand how our family is made up. I'm the oldest boy. Erik is one year younger. Then four years passed before Emory was born, and another four years later came Emil. With Erik, Emory, and Emil all four years apart, they each had room to establish their own identities. But with Erik and I so close together, he was often eclipsed by the recognition I got. I always knew that was frustrating for him. He wanted to be Erik Smith, not "Emmitt Smith's brother."

To complicate matters, Erik played behind me at tailback my senior year. He was a junior by then, he knew he could play, and he wanted to be the man—the featured back on his high school football team. And there I was, the object of his resentment.

Knowing how he felt, I did whatever I could to bridge the gap between us. Maybe that was part of the problem. Maybe Erik didn't want his big brother's help.

Still, I kept trying anyway. How would he feel if I stopped?

And so, during some games my senior year, I took myself out early so Erik could play. Once I moved to fullback down near the goal line, so Erik could play tailback and score the touchdown. I did things like this because we were family, but I also knew how well Erik could run. I'll never forget one game against Pensacola Woodham, when Erik

THE EMMITT ZONE

returned a kickoff straight up the field. As he vanished under the pile, you could tell that someone was still inside there, not going down, just moving the pack, moving the pack, until Erik busted out for a highlight film of a touchdown.

Please don't let me give you a false impression, either: Even when we were fighting, my brother and I were devoted to each other. If I saw another player hit Erik late? I'd try to take that player's head off. I'm not kidding. I saw one guy hit Erik late, and I hunted that joker down and I punished him. I know: Erik could do just fine taking care of himself. But he would do the exact same thing for me. We're blood and that's all there is to it.

If we ever forgot this, even for a moment, our parents used to remind us. One time at spring practice, our team had its annual Orange and Blue intersquad scrimmage. Erik was running the ball and I was playing defense, and I raced up and popped him a good one. My parents couldn't believe it. "Son," my mother told me after the scrimmage, "if you ever hit your brother that hard again, I'm gonna kill ya."

When I graduated from high school, I told Erik and all my brothers the same thing. "The stage is set," I said. "You'll have colleges come and look at you just because you're my brother. Whether you like it or not, that's the reality. So you know you're gonna be looked at. The only thing you have to do now is go to school, get your education, and have a productive year."

Today Erik is more at peace with my success, and this

EMMITT SMITH

has relaxed the way we respond to each other. It isn't one-sided, though. I've done my share of maturing too.

Erik and I are now closer than ever before. That's something I'm thankful for.

■ ■ ■

In my first three years at Escambia High, we'd gone 7–3, 12–2, and 13–1, with two straight state championships. After that type of progress, I was expecting the ultimate senior year: 14–0, another 4-A Florida state title, and the number one ranking in the United States.

I was thinking big, but I wasn't alone. Even before our first game that September, ESPN, *USA Today,* and *Sports Illustrated* had all come to Pensacola for stories on me and my teammates. Our athletic department even got a phone call from Jimmy Breslin, the famous New York columnist. But the season had started by then and Coach Thomas turned him down.

For about eight weeks—before our infamous game against Pensacola High—we *were* sitting on top of the national polls. Football polls, however, sometimes reflect the season before. And, in truth, our team my senior year had lost some strength. Several defensive stars had left for college. We'd also lost Jimmy Nichols, our offensive coordinator, when he took a head coaching job at another high school. Not only was Jimmy Nichols a big-time coach, we also had to learn his successor's new offense.

None of that mattered the night we showed up to play at Pensacola High. This was a time to prove things, not make excuses. Ten thousand people jammed in. Another five or six thousand were turned away. For this game, the hype had been building all season. Both teams were from Pensacola and disliked each other. Pensacola High was known for taking a shortcut or two; we were considered squeaky clean. We were undefeated and they had one loss. Each team desperately wanted to make the state playoffs. But when it comes to the magnitude of this game, I think this says it all: Other local schools moved their games to Thursday night, so everyone in the city could come to ours on Friday.

Early in the first quarter, we scored on a 60-yard bomb from our quarterback, John Brady, to our speedy wide receiver, Marzette Porterfield. When both defenses dug in, we ended up leading at halftime, 10–3.

The biggest play of the game happened in the third quarter. On our own 49-yard line, we had the ball on fourth and 1. We could have punted, tried pinning them near their goal line, but we took a gamble and went for the first down. I took a handoff to the right, bounced outside to the corner, hit the sideline, turned on the jets, and went 51 yards for a backbreaking TD that put us up 17–3.

But the refs called it back.

They said I stepped out-of-bounds.

I did not step out-of-bounds.

In the heat of a play, sometimes a runner can't see where his feet are. I realize that. But on this play I saw the sideline—and I never touched it. After the game, the films showed the same thing. If you ask them at the right time, even some Pensacola players will tell you I stayed in bounds.

EMMITT SMITH

That play killed our team, not theirs. They went on to win 17–10.

It was a classic high school game, but also one full of strangeness. The referees that night were graduates of Pensacola Senior High, which by now had been renamed Pensacola High. In the feverish week before our game on Friday, everyone in town was talking about a game played twenty-five years earlier to that same day. That game's outcome was also controversial. Only that time, Escambia narrowly won. But here, to me, is the most bizarre thing of all: In the biggest high school game this city had ever seen, I carried the ball just twice in the second half.

All-American this and blue-chip that, and I carried the ball *two times*. Calling our plays that game was the offensive coordinator who replaced Jimmy Nichols. I've always wondered myself what was on his mind.

Losing that game hurt our players deeply. In the locker room afterwards, I still recall not wanting to take off my uniform. I just wanted to sit there all night with my teammates. I'm sure there would have been tears under any circumstances. We'd lost a huge game. For the seniors, our high school careers were nearly over. Guys we'd been friends with for life would be going their separate ways. Still, I think our tears were even more heartfelt that night. Since we all felt in our hearts that we had been cheated, I think my teammates and I lost some of our innocence.

We came back our next game and destroyed Pine Forest, our final opponent. Then, for the second time in two weeks, we thought we got robbed. Even though our record was 9–1, we didn't receive a berth to the state playoffs. In the bummer to end all bummers, Pensacola High did.

Once the season ended, the numbers I posted in high school were widely discussed. In four years at Escambia High, I ran for 8,804 yards. I scored 106 touchdowns, while averaging 7.8 yards per carry. I gained more than 100 yards in forty-five of the forty-nine games I played, including the last twenty-eight. And I helped a once-terrible team win two state championships.

This statistic wasn't nearly as well-known, but it's one I'm equally proud of: After four years of high school, I finished in the top hundred of my class.

For the season I had as a senior, *Parade* magazine named me its high school player of the year. People asked me afterwards: "Do you feel this makes you the country's best high school player?" I told them no. With so many outstanding players in this nation, it's impossible to label someone the best. That's mostly a media thing.

This doesn't mean I wasn't grateful, however. I was thrilled to win that award from *Parade*. It honored not only me, but all my high school teammates. In football, you do it together.

6 COLLEGE DAYS

Our fullback, Sam Bettis, had been right. By the end of my sophomore year in high school, letters from college recruiters had started pouring in. By my senior year the thrill had already worn off. The letters were fine, but I was getting up to twelve phone calls a night. Some of the calls would come in as late as 11 P.M. With a full load of classes, I felt myself getting worn out. Just so I could escape and get some rest, some nights I'd sleep at a friend's house. That didn't help my family, though. I might be gone, but the telephone was still ringing.

With the way I performed as a high school player in

Florida, I received offers from just about every major college. Some of the schools were like babies, though. They told me that I wouldn't fit in with their offense, that they never really wanted me. But they said this *after* they knew I wouldn't be going there.

As for the media, I did have a few detractors. One scouting service said I was "a lugger, not a runner. The sportswriters blew him all out of proportion." That one I didn't hear until later on, but there was a guy in Texas whom I was already aware of. A writer for a recruiting magazine, he said I'd be a total flop as a college tailback.

Once I started to narrow the field, I went on several recruiting trips—to Nebraska, Clemson, Florida State, Auburn, and Florida—and all the people I met seemed friendly and honest. My only disturbing trip was to Alabama. I went with a female friend of mine, my close buddy Johnny Nichols, and his girlfriend. After watching Alabama play Penn State, we walked back to a frat house where we'd been instructed to park. There was also a white recruiting coach with us, so I was the only black guy when some white fraternity brothers demanded we move our car. They were rude and obnoxious, and it felt racial to me. But just as I got worked up, the white recruiting coach jumped in these frat guys' faces. I mean, he was wild. Veins were bulging, and he seemed ready to fight the entire fraternity.

I thought: Thanks for watching my back, Coach. But so long, Alabama.

"It was nice meeting you," I told him later that night. "It was nice visiting your university, but I don't think I'll be coming here."

EMMITT SMITH

Some coaches even came to our home, including a pair of famous ones—Auburn's Pat Dye and Florida State's Bobby Bowden. Like all the coaches who visited our house, they tried charming my mom so they could score points with me. But she's a perceptive lady and didn't fall for that stuff. Still, she probably liked Bowden and Dye more than the others. They were just as intent on recruiting me, but they came in straightforward and down-to-earth, without any flash or phony promises. Coach Bowden had one big advantage over Coach Dye, though: My mom didn't want me leaving the state of Florida.

Even though I also liked Coach Bowden, Florida State was never a major contender. I saw the way they rotated their backs, and it didn't exactly thrill me. One week a guy would gain 200 yards, the next week he wasn't starting. I also never felt serious about Miami, even though I knew Jimmy Johnson had a great ball club. The last few seasons, Miami had emphasized Mike Irvin and Vinny Testaverde. Now that Testaverde was leaving, they still had Steve Walsh. I admire a passing game too, but I wanted a team that relied more on its running.

At the end there were three finalists: Auburn, Nebraska, and Florida. "Go wherever you want to," my father told me. "Just make sure you study." My mom voted for Florida, because it was in the state and also for its academics. Just coming off probation, Florida's football program still had a long way to go, but its academics were held in high regard. That was important to our whole family, not just my mother. I was about to become the first Smith to enroll in college.

Having lived my entire life in Pensacola, I also felt a strong attachment to Florida. And for three main reasons, their just-lifted probation was not a major concern. First: I've never understood how the NCAA chooses what schools to punish anyway. With as many crazy rules as the NCAA has, I believe every college bends at least a few. Second: Even if Florida had gotten cited, they had paid for it with probation and now they were starting fresh. Third: As part of its penalty, the NCAA had cut Florida's football scholarships. This meant the talent was good but not great. So I figured I'd get to play a lot as a freshman.

Florida wasn't a lock, though. When I looked at Nebraska, I saw a strong, compassionate coach in Tom Osborne, a consistent national-championship contender, an A-list conditioning program, and an offense with a history of fine runners (Roger Craig, Tom Rathman, Mike Rozier, Johnny Rodgers, and I. M. Hipp, to name just a few).

But Nebraska was too cold and too far from home.

That left Florida and Auburn, and Auburn is actually closer to Pensacola. It's just ninety miles away in southern Alabama, compared to the three hundred miles to Florida's campus in Gainesville. More important than proximity, I *loved* Auburn University. Bo Jackson had won the Heisman while playing running back there; the Auburn people said I could win it there too. I even met Bo himself on my recruiting trip there. He turned out to be a heck of a guy, and he also said nice things about Coach Dye. Bo struck me as honest, too, not somebody who'd mislead a young recruit.

Auburn looked good for other reasons. Their field was grass, their football team loaded with talent. And the fans at Auburn really seemed to want me. In Orlando, Florida, the first week of January, with letter-of-intent day coming next month, I got introduced to the crowd at the Citrus Bowl, where Auburn was playing USC. It was one of the greatest moments of my youth. I was a senior in high school, the Citrus Bowl was jammed, and the Auburn contingent went nuts when I got announced. I literally had goose bumps, and I almost wished my mom were there that night. Then she'd have understood the way I felt about Auburn.

Auburn or Florida?

Florida or Auburn?

Though I'm normally pretty good at making decisions, I couldn't pull the trigger. With one week left to sign, I still hadn't made up my mind, so to quiet the speculation I made an announcement. On the morning of national-letter-signing day, I'd show up at Escambia High in the colors of my next school.

So what did I wear that day?

Nebraska red and white.

With all the attention surrounding my decision, I thought I should inject a little humor. Funny guy, huh?

Actually, I had called both Florida and Auburn the day before I signed—and said I was going with Florida.

I was still grappling right to that final day. But in the end I wanted to please my mom.

■　■　■

As dearly as I loved my family, I was also eighteen years old. I couldn't wait to leave home and assert my independence.

Then, my final semester of high school, my mother's mom passed away. Erik and I went to see her before she died. She couldn't recognize us, and her suffering broke my heart. When that summer came along, leaving home didn't look so enticing anymore. I wanted to stay where I was, in the house on North G Street.

I'll never forget the day I left Pensacola for Gainesville. My parents took their car. I drove a car that my grandpa had bought me as a graduation gift. When we all pulled up to my dorm it was raining outside, and the sadness hit me immediately. Later that day, watching my mom and dad drive away, I never felt more lonely in my whole life. One or two weekends a month the rest of my freshman year, I'd drive almost six hundred miles from Gainesville to Pensacola and back to Gainesville. It was tiring, but worth it. I had never really been away from home.

When Media Day rolled around, it was obvious nobody saw me as just one more homesick freshman. One reporter told me, "People around here are saying you could be the savior. How do you feel about that?"

Though it made me uneasy, I understood where the question came from. I was the high school runner who gained more than 8,000 yards, the local son who stayed loyal to his roots. People in Gainesville expected a lot out of me. But facts were facts. I hadn't even played my first college game, and Florida was part of the SEC, which had some of the best college players in the country. Alabama had Derrick Thomas and Bobby Humphrey. Reggie Cobb played at Tennessee, Harvey Williams at LSU, and Georgia was totally stacked. Rodney Hampton, Tim Worley, Lawrence Tate, and Keith Henderson all played for the Bulldogs.

EMMITT SMITH

I respected those other players and other teams, and I respected my own teammates at Florida. So when I heard the word "savior" at Media Day, I tried cutting off that talk as quickly as possible. "I'm not anyone's savior," I told the writers politely. "There's a lot of guys on this team who can play ball. I'm just here to play my hardest and help the Gators win."

On September 5, 1987, my college career began with a broken promise. Galen Hall was Florida's head coach. Knowing how much I might mean to his program, Galen had recruited me himself. Even now I can still hear the words he said: "If you come to Florida, Emmitt, then I'm gonna start you."

I took that to mean immediately—in our first game at Miami. Starting my first college game? In the packed-out Orange Bowl? How sweet would that be?

Man, was I ticked off. Not only didn't I start, I didn't even play until late in the fourth quarter. By then we were getting pounded. Michael Irvin destroyed us that afternoon, Jimmy Johnson had his whole squad thinking it was unbeatable, and Miami embarrassed us, 31–4. Even today, I still get needled about this by ex-Hurricanes on the Cowboys. Miami's long snapper that game was a guy named Willis McGee. By making two bad snaps that went out of their own end zone, Willis gave us two safeties. Those were our only points that day. So whenever those Miami guys want to tease me, they call that game "Miami 31, Willis McGee 2."

I never complained to Galen Hall. Then one day at practice the following week, he approached me.

"I know you're wondering why I didn't start you at Miami," Galen said. "I thought the pressure might be too much, with their crowd and everything. I didn't want you to make a mistake and lose your confidence."

I said, "Coach, how will you ever know if I'm a good football player if you don't throw me out there in a pressure situation and see how I respond?"

First Galen looked surprised. Then he looked pleased. Then he said he agreed with me and I stopped being angry. He really was a decent man, which was part of the reason I played for him in the first place.

I still didn't start the next week against Tulsa, but I did gain 109 yards and score 2 touchdowns. I think that opened a lot of people's eyes, especially since my first touchdown went 66 yards, Florida's longest TD run since Neal Anderson went for 80 three years earlier. Before becoming a star for the Chicago Bears, Neal had been just as dominating at Florida. And when I broke one for 66 yards my second game in college, the media instantly started making comparisons. In one feature story after that game, the reporter mentioned all four ex-Gators then starting at running back in the NFL: Neal Anderson, Lorenzo Hampton, John L. Williams, and James Jones. Then the reporter said, "Is this the start of the Emmitt Smith Era at Florida?"

We played Alabama next at Legion Field. This is a game I'll hold on to the rest of my life. It was both teams' SEC opener. It was Florida's first game on national television since coming off probation. It was getting built up as a battle between two Heisman candidates—Kerwin Bell for us and Bobby Humphrey for them. I was *dying* to start, but I still didn't know with fifteen minutes to kickoff. Then our coaches announced our lineups in the locker room, and I got what I hoped for: my first college start. Against Alabama. With the game on CBS.

Behind an offensive line that was smoking, I carried 39 times for 2 touchdowns and 224 yards. We upset Alabama, 23–14. And we did it at their place.

After the game, I found out that my 224 yards had broken Florida's single-game yardage record. The old mark had been set in 1930, forty years before I was born.

After my performance at Alabama, everything seemed to accelerate. Just three games into my freshman year, I was already being called a Heisman contender. At our next game, a 38–3 thrashing of Mississippi State, I ran for 3 TDs and 173 yards—and 74,421 Gator fans went crazy. Up in the stands at Florida Field, the college students were calling me "King Emmitt." It was funny. I could see them bowing down like the two guys in *Wayne's World:* We're not worthy, we're not worthy.

Although it felt fantastic, it didn't come as a shock that I played so well this early. The college game was faster, more complex, and more physical. But I played my high school football in Florida, one of college football's most fertile recruiting grounds. Coming from that background, I came to the college game with good self-confidence. But I also wasn't deluded. Because I respected the game and those who played it, I never fooled myself into thinking I could coast.

On October 17, in our seventh game, I passed the 1,000-

yard mark. I did this faster than any runner in college football history. I certainly wasn't shooting for it, though. Until somebody told me I broke it, I had no idea what the record was. Before I came along, the previous record belonged to Tony Dorsett, a person I admired when I was a child. That part of it felt nice. But again, I had no illusions. One day in the future, I was certain, some college back would surpass us all.

With Auburn, Georgia, and Florida State still waiting for us, we lost three of our last four to finish a mediocre 6–5. Due to the strength of our schedule, we still went to the Aloha Bowl in Hawaii, where we all put on grass skirts and hula-danced onstage, where UCLA beat us 20–16, and where I got an early glimpse of some of my future NFL teammates: Troy Aikman, Ken Norton, Jr., Frank Cornish, and James Washington.

With 1,341 yards, eight 100-yard games, and a 5.9-yard average per carry, I finished ninth that year in the Heisman Trophy voting. Almost everyone called this impressive for a freshman. Some people felt more strongly and said I should have won it.

I wasn't sure how to feel. True, I was a freshman, and seniors normally win it. But that season there weren't many senior standouts. If they did pick a senior, I thought Lorenzo White of Michigan State was most deserving. He produced, all year, and the Big Ten's a tough conference.

Instead, a junior won that year's Heisman: Tim Brown of Notre Dame. I couldn't believe it when I found out. As explosive as he was, Tim Brown was a wide receiver and punt returner. From all my years of watching college football, I thought the Heisman winner needed to be the workhorse, a team's primary weapon for all four quarters and not just a handful of times each game.

For all I know, Tim Brown may be the nicest man in the world. Obviously, I have nothing against him personally. But I did think the Heisman voters blew it that season. A lot of football fans did.

■ ■ ■

In the spring of my freshman year, after football season ended, I received the first bad press of my college career. Which also made it the first bad press of my life.

One night, some offensive linemen at Florida were at the same frat party I was. I left those guys to check out another party. When I returned to the first one about an hour later, I saw a crowd of angry people outside. It was my teammates and several of my freshman brothers, bickering with some frat guys. I tried cooling down my freshman brothers, but then one of the frat guys said something to one of our guys, and suddenly he was enraged. I finally pulled him away, toward my car parked at the curb. I had my front door open. He was walking around to the passenger seat. I was yelling out to the rest of our freshman brothers, "Come on, let's go. Y'all don't need to be getting in trouble."

Just then, a frat guy walked up to me. Definitely drunk and possibly a bigot, he cursed me out and told me to move my car. When I didn't, he called me a nigger.

I didn't punch him. Even if I wanted to—and part of me did—I couldn't do much that night anyway: a couple days before this, lifting weights, I'd pulled the pectoral muscle on my right side.

So I simply placed my forearm in front of his neck and slowly moved him back, out of my face. Before this could escalate, or not escalate, one of my freshman brothers came flying over the trunk of my car. He cracked this guy in the face. The guy fell in the street, and somebody saw him lying there. All his fraternity brothers came running over, and now everyone was fighting and stopping traffic.

I still hadn't thrown a punch, but those were my freshman brothers mixing it up. Something strange happened then. Just as I was getting ready to tangle, the fight lost all its steam. I still don't know what happened. Maybe everyone saw a police car cruising by.

We all jumped in our cars and went back to our dorm. But we couldn't let it go. Our guys were saying, "Hey, man, *they* picked this fight. *They* started this. We gotta go back and finish it."

So then we did what football players do: We rounded up more football players. We ended up with twelve, which still left us outnumbered, but we didn't care. We went straight back there and cleaned *house*. This was the racial mix: All the frat guys were white; eight of our twelve guys were white and four were black. And when one of their white guys said to one of our black guys, "I want you one-on-one, nigger," that white guy got blasted. All our guys got a huge laugh out of that. Black or white, we were all Gators.

The rest of it wasn't so funny. A few of the frat guys got taken away in an ambulance. Two of my freshman brothers were arrested. When the story hit the papers, one headline began: "EMMITT SMITH AND 11 OTHERS . . ."

It made me sound like the ringleader. And I never hit anyone!

The media dubbed us the Dirty Dozen. It turned into national news. I had to call my parents and tell them what really happened.

■　■　■

By that September, with everyone getting enthused about college football, the Dirty Dozen was mostly forgotten, and Florida was hyping me as a major Heisman contender. But even before our first game my sophomore year, I saw there might be problems for our entire offense. When a new offensive coordinator comes in, a period of adjustment always follows. It can be fairly quick, or it can take a few seasons. It mostly depends on how foreign the incoming system is.

In this case, our new offensive coordinator was a coach named Lynn Amedee. Coming to Florida from Texas A&M, he brought about fifty-eight offensive formations with him. I'm all for diversity, but I thought that was overdoing it just a tad. To my surprise, he also decided to stress the passing game. Don't get me wrong: I've always liked catching passes, and Coach Amedee made certain that I did. But our quarterback, Kerwin Bell, had just graduated. Our offensive line blocked best for the run. As a freshman, I had led the SEC in rushing. So I couldn't quite understand Coach Amedee's rationale. That's what happened, though. Our offense my second year was geared for the pass.

THE EMMITT ZONE

In two easy nonconference games, we destroyed Montana State 69–0 and Indiana State 58–0. On the other hand, we also beat three SEC teams, including 14th-ranked LSU. Even with Florida at 5–0 and ranked 14th in the country, I still wasn't in love with our new offense, but I was excited for us as a team. With Memphis State and Vanderbilt coming up next, I thought we could handle them both and be 7–0.

In game six, against Memphis State, I went down with a knee injury. Running into the hole, I got stood up at the line of scrimmage. As I relaxed my legs—when I should've kept them moving—a defender drove his shoulder into the back of my knee. I heard something pop and knew my day was over.

When I saw a tape of the play, I told myself, "You should have known better than that," because Walter Payton was one of my childhood heroes. Later, in high school, some people said we had similar running styles. A couple of girls even called me by Walter's nickname, Sweetness. And when I was a kid, the one thing that struck me about Walter Payton—even more than his talent and heart—were those pumping legs of his. Walter's legs *never* stopped moving, and I always wanted to follow his example, and normally I did.

Reality set in hard after I got hurt. Dating all the way back to peewee league, I'd never missed a game because of an injury. And after all those years of good health and good fortune, I thought I was invincible. Looking back on it now, this was ridiculous.

Even those first two days after I got injured, I was still

telling myself my knee was fine. Then, one night in my dorm room, I tried running down our hall and my knee gave out. The pain was profound, but not as profound as the message it sent. My parents and Coach Thomas had always told me: "Football could end any moment. But your education will last your entire life." I always knew they were right, and I never ignored my schoolwork. But that night when I felt my knee buckle under me, it cemented my commitment to my education. Football *could* end in a heartbeat, and it could end for any reason, like not pumping my legs for one split second.

Our team doctor told me the knee was "stable." This meant it wouldn't need to be surgically reconstructed, which is every athlete's worst nightmare. I had only stretched a ligament, he said; I should be playing again in four to six weeks.

I wanted to believe him. Injured knees have ended people's careers.

I couldn't believe him, though. At least not completely. My knee felt all torn up.

It was awful. One minute I told myself, "You'll be back. The doctor said so and he's the expert." Then I'd tell myself, "Wake up, fool. It's over."

The next few weeks were stressful and depressing. But I knew I'd make things worse if I let this affect my classwork. I've seen it happen: A college athlete gets injured, gets down on himself, and starts blowing off going to school. I was frustrated, too, but I wasn't about to let that happen.

So rather than go on the road with the football team, I

THE EMMITT ZONE

stayed at home and spent extra time with my books. When I did interact with our team, in one respect I found it disillusioning. My teammates were great, hanging out with me on campus, calling me on the phone, letting me know I was still one of the guys. The feeling I got from our coaches was utterly different. When I'd run into them, they didn't have much to say, and they never looked me in the eye. What was that all about? Now that I couldn't produce, they could care less about me? It really hurt me, because some of the coaches, I thought, were also my friends.

But it didn't hurt me for long. If a true friend lets you down, that's worth feeling lousy about. If it's someone only pretending, you just face facts and move on.

Once I got over feeling depressed, I tried taking a similar attitude toward my knee injury. So I just kept moving forward, just kept showing up at the swimming pool each day, even though I'm not exactly the Swimming King. It was the physical therapist's idea. He said running each day in deep water would strengthen my knee.

"How deep water?" I asked.

"About fifteen feet," he said.

Hello? I thought he was dipping into his own medications.

But once they put those seven life vests on me—okay, it was two—I started enjoying my rehab sessions. I liked the results I saw. I liked overcoming one of my fears.

Probably the roughest week that month was the one when we played Vanderbilt. I was at a friend's house, watching my teammates lose on TV. Even worse, the game was in Nashville, and the Vanderbilt players were doing some heavy taunting. I could feel my blood pressure rising, and I kept saying out loud to my friend's TV set, "Next year you come to us! Next year you'll pay! I'll run all over y'all when you come up here!"

We lost 24–9, our first conference defeat. After a bye week we lost to Auburn, and by the following week I felt ready to play. For all my anxieties, the doctor's diagnosis was right on the money: I had been out exactly four weeks.

At my first day of practice before my comeback, I was determined not to baby my knee. I wanted to know, for real, if it could withstand an actual game. Still, I wasn't reckless. Before running all out, I carefully checked out the knee, and it felt fine. In fact, *both* my legs felt stronger than ever before. I also felt quicker and faster! The therapist knew his stuff—the swimming pool had worked like a dream.

Wearing a knee brace, I carried 19 times that Saturday against Georgia. But their swarming defense held me to 68 yards, and they won 26–3. After we beat Kentucky, Florida State demolished us 52–17 in their ear-splitting Doak Campbell Stadium. The final score was galling enough; on top of that, Florida State was our hottest rival. This particular game, there was nearly a fight before the opening kickoff. I never saw how it started, but both teams were suddenly standing at midfield, pointing fingers and jabbering. Meanwhile, their Seminole Indian mascot tried riding on his horse through the 50-yard line. He wanted to throw down his stake, right at midfield, but he rode into a mob and flew off his horse. The guy wasn't hurt and the whole crowd cracked up.

THE EMMITT ZONE

This was also the first game I played without my knee brace. In the second half, I took a shot to the knee that hampered my running. Nothing serious, just painful. With our offense also passing to try to catch up, I wound up with just 15 carries for 56 yards. Having missed two other games completely, I ended the season with 988 yards. Ever since I was a freshman in high school, I had never missed 1,000. I'd never even come close.

That was how my sophomore season went. My entire life, I'd never had less fun while playing football. My knee injury was only part of it. As our team lost five of our last six games, player-coach relations got more and more strained. I felt Lynn Amedee, in particular, did a lot of finger-pointing. He kept blaming our offensive players for not being "smart" enough to pick up his new system. I thought that was horse manure, and also unseemly.

After one of our losses, the coaches called a meeting to "clear the air." So one of our wide receivers, Willie Snead, stood up and spoke freely. "Everything starts in the front office," Willie said. "When the front office isn't stable, it trickles down to the team. We, as players, must get our acts together. But so do the coaches."

I felt this took guts—exactly what coaches want their players to have. And yet, at our very next practice, Willie got demoted to second team.

A bad situation only got uglier. "That's exactly what we mean," we told our coaches. "You ask us our opinion. We give it to you, you don't like what you hear, and you punish us."

A football team might not be a democracy, but it

shouldn't be a dictatorship. But, oddly enough, we'd have all been better off with a *more* controlling head coach. Galen Hall, a quiet, dignified man, was too calm, in my opinion. He should have taken command. Instead, he let his assistants run the show.

Even with our second straight 6–5 season, we went to the All-American Bowl in Birmingham, Alabama, where we won 14–10 against Jeff George and Illinois. This game was very satisfying for me, because Illinois came in bragging. Their general rap to the press was, "Emmitt Smith hasn't been hit this year. Now he'll see what it's like to get hit by a Big Ten team."

It was cold that December night in Birmingham, and I had the flu, but I wasn't about to miss this one. The teams I respect most are the ones who just play football. They don't use the press to try to intimidate me.

I didn't waste any time. On our first offensive play, I took a toss left and got around the corner. Then I ran past all their pursuit for a 55-yard touchdown. Rushing for another TD and 159 yards, I ended up being named our Most Valuable Player. I felt I had made my point. The Big Ten is strong, but so is the SEC.

It was good to end this frustrating year with a win. It couldn't fix everything, though. Our football program was still heading for trouble.

7
CONFLICT AND DECISIONS

A s I started my junior season, for the third time in three years we had a different offensive coordinator. I wasn't pleased when I heard the news, as this isn't exactly a sign of a football program's stability. It also meant starting from scratch, again, on another new offense.

But I like to keep an open mind, and I felt much better the moment I met Whitey Jordan. Whitey seemed like a guy who cared about his players, and he clearly knew the running game. In his previous job, at SMU, he had coached Eric Dickerson and Craig James.

When one reporter asked Whitey how I compared to

Eric, he said: "Eric was faster, bigger. But Emmitt has more moves. He knows how to make people miss, so nobody gets a solid lick on him. Emmitt has the strongest legs and best vision of any back I've been around."

That was extremely nice to hear. So was Whitey's promise to get me the football. So I started my junior year feeling happy. I felt I could be a pure runner, something I'd wanted my whole career in college.

With Whitey Jordan behind me, I started out on a roll. In our opening loss to Mississippi, I rushed for 117 yards and 2 touchdowns (setting a Florida school record with my fifteenth 100-yard game). In our next two games, both wins, I had 3 more TDs and 282 yards. In that third game, against Memphis State, my parents were in the stands. After one of my touchdowns, they saw me do an end zone celebration. Even back then, this wasn't my style. But Memphis State had been talking noise all day. So had their raucous fans during pregame warm-ups.

My father didn't care about any of that. That night he told me, "Son, you don't need to be doing that type of thing. That's not the image you're trying to get across. You've been in the end zone so many times. Why are you acting like you've never seen one?"

He was right, and he was also my father. I've never really celebrated since.

After shutting out Mississippi State the next week, we went into Baton Rouge for a thrilling last-second win over LSU. As time expired, our sophomore kicker, Arden Czyzewski, kicked a long field goal, and we came from behind to beat LSU 16–13. It was one of those games that bring a ball club together. Not only did we win at Tiger Stadium—maybe the noisiest, rowdiest place I've ever played—but a lot of different people made contributions. Tim Paulk blocked a punt that set up a field goal. Our linebacker, Huey Richardson, had 4 sacks and 19 tackles. As a unit, our defense held their all-SEC quarterback Tommy Hodson to under 200 yards passing. They also intercepted 3 of his passes.

Our locker room after that game was charged with emotion. This was our fourth straight win, and we'd gotten it on the road in hostile conditions. While addressing our team, Galen Hall even shed a few tears.

The following day, we found out the real reason why Coach Galen was so choked up.

On Sunday we had a team meeting at 4 P.M. Just before it began, our players were all downstairs in our meeting room, watching pro football on the big-screen TV. We suddenly saw Brent Musburger on the screen. He was making a special announcement. Behind him, as everybody got quiet, a network graphic read: The University of Florida.

"Excuse this interruption," Brent Musburger said. "The University of Florida has announced that Galen Hall has resigned as the head coach of the football program."

Our first reaction was shock. Our record was 4–1. We just beat LSU. With Whitey Jordan calling the plays, our offense was averaging 26 points a game. In total defense, our team was ranked number two in the country. After two disappointing seasons of 6–5, we seemed to be on our way. Why would Galen quit now?

THE EMMITT ZONE

After our shock, we felt insulted. Why did we hear it like this? Couldn't they tell the players before they went to the media? That's all the respect for us the athletic department could muster?

The whole situation was murky. And I can't speak for everyone on our team, but many of us believed that Galen had no choice. We felt they may have forced him out. Dick Arnsparger, our athletic director, had formerly been head coach at LSU. This season there had been speculation all over campus that Arnsparger may have had designs on Galen Hall's job.

As a player, I tried ignoring the distractions. When I did think about them, I never dreamed there'd be a change during midseason. I didn't want a coaching change, either. Even though he could've been tougher with us, I'd always felt affection for Galen Hall. He was one of the reasons I came to Florida.

Even today, I don't know the true story behind Galen's resignation. I'm guessing that I probably never will.

■ ■ ■

There were other clouds hanging over our football team that fall. The NCAA was on our campus, investigating the Florida basketball team. With the NCAA people hanging around, there was speculation that football was also getting looked at. As it later turned out, the NCAA did put the football team on probation, for violations occurring while Galen Hall was its coach.

So, did the threat of probation contribute to Galen's losing his job?

EMMITT SMITH

Again, it's hard to say. For one thing, the sanctions weren't handed down until Galen had been gone for nearly one year. Either way, I've been told that his transgressions were relatively minor, having more to do with his heart than with his ambition. Evidently, Galen helped out one of his players and one of his coaches, and the NCAA called his actions a violation.

When the verdict finally came down, I wasn't surprised. With as many arcane rules as the NCAA has, I don't see how any college can be pristine. And I still don't quite comprehend their method of enforcement. How do they choose which schools to punish, and which to leave alone?

You know what else I find strange? Once the NCAA files charges against a program, it almost appears that program must prove what it *didn't* do. That's slightly backwards, isn't it? In the American legal system, innocence is presumed until someone is proven guilty.

I also think the NCAA is out of line on the issue of the Black Coaches Association. Let me give you my viewpoint. When the NCAA chose not to add one extra scholarship to the thirteen allowed each school for its basketball team, the BCA threatened to boycott one weekend of games. It was a host of issues, not just this one, but this was the flash point, and I thought the BCA was right on. With the type of profit made by college athletics, how much could one more scholarship hurt? How can you lose by giving one more kid, probably a black kid, a chance to get a college education?

I don't understand the NCAA's thinking, just as I don't understand why, year after year, the NCAA keeps raising academic standards for incoming student-athletes. What exactly is gained by denying these kids educational opportunities?

I think it's pretty clear what can be lost. Look at all the promising kids from the inner cities, kids with no access to higher education. Some of those bright young kids go to school on the street. Some end up in jail or dead. That may sound harsh, but sometimes life is.

While I'm getting this stuff off my chest, I have another beef with the NCAA. They have thousands and thousands of rules and regulations. They have them, they say, in the name of protecting "amateur athletics."

Now wait a minute. From where I stand that's total hypocrisy. Amateur athletics? College sports is a multimillion-dollar business. And with all those millions of dollars changing hands, the athletes don't receive any compensation. I find this amazing. In a huge, huge business—probably bigger than even the NFL, since there's so many more college teams than pro—the labor force doesn't get paid. The people who generate most of the media interest, the network TV money, the pay-per-view money, the postseason bowl money, the people who break their bones and limbs, have to stand around like dopes and work for free, while everyone else keeps raking in the green.

Why?

Because the NCAA says so.

What I want to know is, Who are these people to make decisions like that? Why do they have so much power? And how much money do their executives make?

EMMITT SMITH

When I played at Florida, I used to look in the stands before our home games. Our stadium held about 75,000 people, and every week it would sell out or come close. As a football player, it was wonderful to see all those people cheering. I'll never forget how incredible that felt.

But I was more than a football player. I was also a college student—a student who couldn't work during football season, because the NCAA wouldn't allow it. So most of the time, I was lucky if I had twenty bucks in my pocket. And sometimes I couldn't help thinking when I looked into our stands: There are thousands of fans wearing Florida jerseys today, with my number 22 across the front. There are thousands more wearing T-shirts reading: RUN, EMMITT, RUN, and CATCH 22, IF YOU CAN. I'm not Donald Trump, but I know serious profit when I see it. But if I were to take some initiative, create my own small corporation, print and sell my own T-shirts bearing my name and likeness, the NCAA would call it a "violation."

I don't get it. Whatever happened to capitalism? Or basic American rights?

The NCAA is always evaluating others. I think it's time to evaluate the NCAA. It's a powerful institution, a powerful group of people with impact on many young lives. Perhaps it's out of touch with modern society. Perhaps education experts should put their heads together with experts on athletics, and figure out how to implement some change. In fact, I hope to make a difference myself in this area someday.

■ ■ ■

THE EMMITT ZONE

On October 8, my teammates and I had learned about Galen Hall's resignation. Although stunned by the news, we had a game against Vanderbilt in six days.

When Saturday came, I did what I think I've always been good at: I kept my focus and ran as hard as ever.

I also came into that game with some extra motivation. The season before, in Nashville, Vanderbilt was the team that was taunting my teammates. While watching that game on TV with my injured knee, I had promised myself to get even when they came to Gainesville. Now that day was here, and by halftime I had 119 yards. I finished with 202 on 25 carries. With our new interim coach, Gary Darnell, we won 34–11.

That made it five straight wins, despite all the chaos. But this was one of those seasons that just kept getting more bizarre. After the Vanderbilt game, our quarterback, Kyle Morris, was temporarily taken off the team. So was our backup quarterback and a few other players.

Within two weeks, we lost our head coach, our starting quarterback, and his replacement. Our players were walking around asking, "What's next?" I was demoralized too, but not as much as some of our players were. A couple of them were thinking of changing schools.

After Vanderbilt came New Mexico, at home, and the biggest statistical day of my college career. With our top two quarterbacks gone, and a true freshman quarterback rushed into the lineup, the burden swung to me and the running game, and I had myself a career day. Breaking my own Florida single-game rushing record, I ran for 316 yards and 3 touchdowns.

EMMITT SMITH

The funny thing was, I was tired that game and wanted to come out. But New Mexico kept scoring—we beat them 27–21—so I had to keep going out there. What also stands out for me is the phone call I received later from Neal Anderson. With 33 touchdowns in my career, and 3,457 yards, I had just broken two of Neal's all-time school records. When he called me to say congratulations, I thought it was very gracious, but not at all surprising. By then we'd already met and I knew how classy he was.

We ended my junior year our usual way. We defeated Kentucky, then lost to Auburn, Georgia, and Florida State. They were the SEC powers, and we never beat them once while I was at Florida. Even today, with two Super Bowl rings, I still can't think about that without getting all burned up.

But at least my junior year we played those teams tough. We lost by 3 to Auburn, 7 to Georgia, and 7 to Florida State. The Auburn loss was the hardest for me to take. With our first two quarterbacks out, Auburn had no respect for our passing game, and most of the night they came out in a nine-man front. On the snap of the ball, even their cornerbacks were drifting off our receivers. Then they would also come charging into our backfield.

Ever try running a sweep in a game like that?

But our own defense was nasty that night too, and with twenty-six seconds left, it looked as if we'd beat Auburn 7–3. Then something peculiar happened. On fourth down and 11 at our 25, their quarterback, Reggie Slack, found a guy who was wide open. Reggie hit him for 25 yards and the winning TD, the Auburn fans went nuts, and our team felt punched in the gut. All night we'd played brilliant defense. One monumental lapse and Auburn got us again.

Our regular season ended at 7–4, then Washington blew us out in the Freedom Bowl. Later that week another bombshell landed: Whitey Jordan was leaving. Most of our other coaches lost their jobs too. Because rather than retaining Gary Darnell, our interim coach, the athletic department was hiring Steve Spurrier. And Spurrier came in fresh, with a whole new staff.

Hearing that Whitey was going came as a jolt. I loved him both as a person and as a coach, and I thrived under his system. As a junior I'd just completed my finest season. I gained 1,599 yards, leading the SEC and setting a new Florida record. I averaged 5.6 yards per carry, and 145.4 yards per game. In nine of eleven games, I rushed for more than 100 yards. *Sports Illustrated* called me a "yardage machine."

Without Whitey Jordan? His love of the running game and his expertise? It probably wouldn't have happened.

Until Whitey left, I had no intentions of leaving college early. But that's when I started to give it serious thought. Suddenly I was asking myself tough questions, and I didn't have much time to make decisions. Washington blew us out on December 30, 1989. In April of 1990, for the first time in history, the NFL would open its draft to college juniors.

Looking ahead to my senior year at Florida, did I want to play for another offensive coordinator? This would mean four in four years, something I never saw coming when I was recruited by Florida. If you look at the schools in this country who have a winning tradition, they all have various styles, but something they share is stability. Florida never had that when I was there.

There was also the threat of probation I talked about earlier (which would actually come to pass that following September). In my senior year, did I want to play for a team that was banned from TV and from bowl games?

It wasn't even close to being the biggest issue, but I also couldn't ignore the question of money. Should I play one more year for free, risk getting badly injured and losing my shot at the pros? Or should I enter the NFL, where I could secure my future and also my family's?

Before making up my mind, I wanted to talk to Steve Spurrier. He would be my coach if I came back my senior year. We had never even met, and I wanted to see what impression I got of him. I also thought I should find out if he *wanted* me to stay.

But Spurrier never asked me to stay at Florida. He never said, "Let's work together. Let's make this a great season." He never even said, "I want you to stay, but I'll understand if you go to the NFL. With the draft open to juniors, I know it must be tempting. So I'm not going to pressure you to stay."

Spurrier, instead, basically told me he needed me to make a decision, because there were guys he was recruiting who might be on the fence.

Maybe I was wrong, but I took that to mean: These high school guys are runners, and they won't come to Florida if you stay. So I need to know what to tell them.

This left me with a cold feeling inside. I also thought it was strange. It wasn't as if I was known as a troublemaker.

THE EMMITT ZONE

It wasn't as if I didn't produce. But Spurrier seemed more concerned about recruiting than he did about making the school's all-time leading rusher feel welcome. And I still don't understand that.

That January, as I increasingly leaned toward the NFL, the more and more anxious I felt about my mom. At first, I didn't even tell her that leaving school was an option. I didn't tell anyone. I wanted to do the research, evaluate my options, then make this important decision on my own.

When I did confide in my mom, I felt tremendous relief. I knew how much she emphasized education, and I feared her disappointment. But my mom agreed that it seemed like time to move on. She was frustrated, too, with the turmoil at Florida. My mother also knew how determined I was. When I told her I'd earn those last credits and get my bachelor's degree, she never doubted my word.

■ ■ ■

On the afternoon of January 31, I called a press conference on the Florida campus. Earlier that morning, other students had kept asking me what I intended to do. I told everyone they'd just have to wait. I wanted to break the news to my teammates first, especially those from the class of 1987. They were my freshman brothers, the guys I came in with.

A few minutes before the press conference, I walked with several teammates out to our football stadium. They were telling me not to leave, but I said my mind was made up. They told me they understood and that I had their support. But their faces still said "stay," and I felt myself getting choked up.

EMMITT SMITH

At the press conference I got emotional again. My football career hadn't turned out the way I envisioned. I'm sure my teammates felt the same way about theirs. Florida's football program up to then was such a revolving door, none of our players could fully develop their talents. But football was only one part of going to college. As I looked around the press conference that day, I saw dozens of people who really mattered to me. It struck me, then, just how much I'd miss this university, and that I was leaving behind a precious part of my life. That's when my eyes filled with tears.

I wasn't going anywhere yet, though. With almost four months of school left our second semester, I was looking forward to simply being a student. I quickly found out I was kidding myself. My leaving school was such big news on campus, some people could not let it go. Some people kept insisting I *had* to come back as a senior: This was my chance for the Heisman. I understood their point of view, but by then I felt the Heisman was highly political. Despite the season I had my junior year, I had only finished seventh in the balloting. Evidently, my performance mattered less than the turbulence at Florida.

Believe it or not, some people felt betrayed when I left Florida. My rookie year with the Cowboys, I even received some hate mail from Gainesville. In one man's letter he called me a nigger, cursed me out, and told me I couldn't play football to begin with. I didn't let that hurt me. I didn't even use it as fuel. I read that man's letter and I felt sorry for him. I couldn't imagine living with that much poison inside me.

THE EMMITT ZONE

8
HIGH
ANXIETY

The NFL draft is where dreams are made.

It's also where they get derailed.

In the course of my three years at Florida, I had teammates who told me: "I'm going in the first round. My agent told me I will. He says I'll be making a million dollars a year."

Some of those college players never even got drafted. I'd see them after the draft and they looked crushed.

That's why I always tell college athletes who ask me about the draft: Don't let anyone fill your head with promises and predictions. They might be setting you up for disappointment. Believe you'll be drafted the moment you hear the announcement.

■ ■ ■

On Draft Day of April 1990, I had no earthly idea what team would choose me. Yes, I heard all the rumors: Seattle, with two early picks in the opening round, wanted me badly. So did Tampa Bay, which was picking fourth. Not only did they need a runner, my Florida background could help them sell more tickets.

I didn't buy into *any* of that. With thirty-eight college juniors coming out early—in addition to all those seniors— this would be one of the deepest drafts in NFL history. On the defensive side alone, there was Junior Seau, Cortez Kennedy, Mark Carrier, Anthony Smith, and Keith Mc-Cants. Just at the running back spot, there was Rodney Hampton, Barry Foster, Blair Thomas, Dexter Carter, and the two Thompsons from the Big Ten, Darrell from Minnesota and Anthony from Indiana. At quarterback there was Jeff George and Andre Ware.

So I truly had no inkling where I would be drafted, and also no serious preferences. I wasn't one of those guys who write letters to NFL teams before the draft, saying, "Don't even think about it. You'll never sign me anyway." I just wanted to be drafted, hopefully by a team where I could start as a rookie.

Like any college player about to turn pro, I did have some question marks by my name. My strength was never an issue. Ever since I was a sophomore in high school, I bench-pressed 280. By my first day of college, I leg-pressed 800. Nevertheless, some critics still called me "too small" at 5-9½. That wasn't the knock I heard most, though. My "lack of breakaway speed" was.

EMMITT SMITH

I felt this was silly. If I got to the end zone, did it matter how many tenths of a second it took? And what about traits like focus, heart, and resilience? I've yet to see a statistic that measures them.

On the question of my speed, one *Sports Illustrated* writer even called up my mom. She told him, "Yes, they talked about his speed. Well, they never saw what he was capable of. They never saw all those ninety-yard runs of his in the peewee leagues. I never did see anyone catch him from behind once he had a ball under his arm."

Thank you, Mama.

Thank you, too, Jimmy Johnson. In a different article in *Sports Illustrated,* Jimmy once said: "There were all these people saying, 'He's too slow,' or 'He's too small.' All I know is that every time I saw a film of him, he was running 50, 60, 70, 80 yards for a touchdown. That looked pretty good to me."

But in April of 1990, I wasn't even thinking about the Cowboys. They had the twenty-first pick and I hoped to be gone by then. Also, after sending a coach to Gainesville to see me work out, the Cowboys had never called me. *No NFL teams were calling me,* and I was becoming a nervous wreck. The night before the draft, I stayed in my old bedroom at my parents' house. But even in those familiar surroundings, I barely slept.

On Sunday morning, I watched the draft on ESPN at a friend's house on Pensacola Beach. Several family members were with me too. Jeff George went first, to the Colts. Then the Jets took Penn State running back Blair Thomas. I'd seen Blair play and I thought he was good. For the East Coast connection, I also knew the Jets liked that he came from Penn State. People were also saying that Blair was faster than me. So once and for all, I'd like to set the record straight. I was not bothered at all when Blair Thomas went before me.

With picks three through six, Cortez Kennedy went to Seattle, Keith McCants to Tampa Bay, Junior Seau to the Chargers, and Mark Carrier to the Bears. That was four straight defensive players, and it seemed to be the theme of the day's first round. When the Patriots, picking tenth, took defensive end Ray Agnew, I walked out of my friend's house. I couldn't watch one more minute, I was so anxious.

Staring out at the Gulf, I let all these negative thoughts invade my head. Maybe I won't be drafted at all. Maybe I should have stayed in college. Maybe I just made the biggest mistake of my life.

Ten long minutes later, I heard my mother calling my name. I had a telephone call, she said.

For a moment I just stood there, not getting excited. Earlier that morning, the telephone rang and everyone jumped. It turned out to be my brother.

But my mom said, "Come on, come on," so I hurried inside.

I picked up the phone and the man said, "This is Bob Ackles, player personnel director of the Dallas Cowboys. Emmitt, how would you like to be a Dallas Cowboy?"

"I'd *love* to be a Dallas Cowboy," I said.

Bob asked for my agent's number, then told me they'd call me right back. By then the first round was up to pick sixteen, and only four offensive players had gotten drafted. Even the Cowboys, picking twenty-first, had been talking up their desire for an impact player on defense. That might have been true or it might have been a smoke screen, so I still didn't know how much this phone call meant. I'd also heard about teams calling up players, telling them they were getting ready to draft them, and then not following through. It's just the nature of Draft Day. Things can change in a instant with all the wheeling and dealing.

Five minutes later the phone rang again. This time I heard the voice of Jimmy Johnson. After introducing himself, Jimmy said, "Emmitt, how would you like to wear a star on your helmet?"

I was so overwhelmed I could barely think. So I just repeated myself. "Coach, I'd *love* to wear a star on my helmet!"

"Good, because we're about to draft you," Jimmy said. "Be ready. We'll call you back in a few minutes to make some flight arrangements. We want you in Dallas tonight."

I told the entire room: "That was the Cowboys again! They say they're about to draft me!"

Everybody went crazy. Then we all heard it together on ESPN. The Cowboys had traded up from their twenty-first spot, to pick me seventeenth.

Just like that, my life had changed in an instant, and all my friends and family were hugging and crying and laughing and running outside to tell neighbors. I felt so much emotion myself, I looked at my hands and they were actually trembling.

■ ■ ■

THE EMMITT ZONE

With almost no time to pack, guess what I wore that night when I stepped off the plane in Dallas? Purple shorts sprinkled with gold polka dots, a matching vest, a gold shirt beneath the vest, a pair of black loafers without socks, a white Cowboys cap, and a gold earring.

You think the press had any fun with that the next day?

That night at the airport, a limousine drove me straight to a crowded press conference, where I said my childhood heroes were Walter Payton and Tony Dorsett, my favorite childhood team was the Dallas Cowboys, and I had no idea the current Cowboys would draft me, I didn't know much about them, but I felt the team would be improved from last year. Some of the media laughed at that final part. The Cowboys were 1–15 the season before. I wasn't exactly going out on a limb.

I also met Jerry Jones and Jimmy Johnson, and they both seemed delighted. Jerry told the media, "This is a bright spot. It's going to make Nate Newton block better, make Troy throw better, and make that defense a lot better, having this guy on our squad."

Jimmy said, "Emmitt Smith brings star quality to us."

Joe Brodsky, Jimmy's backfield coach at Miami and also with the Cowboys, said, "Emmitt Smith will take your breath away. You might not get it back until he scores."

Later that night when the press conference ended, I stepped inside Texas Stadium for the first time. The field was still covered with plywood boards for a tractor pull they were having later that week, but the stadium still looked gorgeous, with one single spotlight illuminating the darkness, and I felt all my childhood memories flooding back. I really was *here*. In *Dallas*. About to play for the *Cowboys*. As I looked around at the names in the Ring of Honor—Roger the Dodger and all the rest—I said to myself: "One day I'll have my name with those other legends up there."

I know, I know: I can get sentimental. But at that perfect moment, who wouldn't?

I also went on radio and TV shows, where everyone seemed thrilled to have me joining the Cowboys. I didn't know it until later, but Jerry Jones also went on a radio show that night. Evidently, the Cowboys never thought they'd be able to draft me. Because going into the draft, Jerry Jones said on the radio, they had me rated "fourth overall" on their list.

Once my agent and I found out what Jerry said, we reminded him of it at the bargaining table. But that would come later. My first night in Dallas was purely one of goodwill.

■　■　■

The week after the draft, I went to the first of the Cowboys' three noncontact quarterback schools. After then returning immediately to Gainesville, where I finished my semester, I reported directly back to Dallas. By then it was May and I still didn't have a contract, but this was not unusual. Andre Ware, Junior Seau, and Blair Thomas all hadn't signed yet either. The season before this, Barry Sanders hadn't signed until September.

But I had no intention of waiting that long. I wanted to

sign by mid-July, when training camp began, and since it was only May I thought we could get it done. In the meantime, I attended our second and third quarterback schools. When I did come to terms with the Cowboys, this would ensure that I already knew our offense.

My first few weeks in Dallas were quite an adjustment. The biggest thing that struck me was all the cowboys. I'd never seen so many of them in one city, and I'd never seen any black cowboys at all. I was also shocked by all the Dallas highways. To a young man coming from Pensacola and Gainesville, they seemed to stretch from here to forever.

Having just turned twenty years old, I also wasn't about to stay locked up in my apartment. Though I still didn't have much money, since I hadn't signed yet, I had taken out a loan and bought a new Datsun 300ZX. That first summer in Dallas, I'd take off the T-top at night and drive all over. I got lost a lot, but I slowly discovered Dallas. And I still recall how nice those warm summer nights felt.

I mostly hung out with two other new Cowboys, James Washington and Vinson Smith. James taught me how to play dominoes, which I still like playing today with my Cowboy teammates. I was also with James my first night on the town, which did not turn out at all how we expected.

Wanting to hit a club we'd been hearing about, James knew only one way to get us there. So he drove us down in his white, big-model Mercedes. Neither one of us knew it, but the street we were on at the time was known for its prostitution. So there we were driving slowly, scanning the streets for this club, when suddenly two black policemen pulled us over. Immediately, they had their hands on their guns.

One officer asked James: "Do you have any weapons in this car?"

James said he had a knife.

James grew up in south-central Los Angeles, where he saw tremendous promise but also a lot of violence. His first summer in Dallas—also at times a dangerous city—I imagine that James felt safer having a knife in his car.

It all happened fast.

James said he had a knife.

The officers got edgy.

One of them ordered James out of the car.

His partner ran around to where I was sitting.

Now both their guns were drawn.

I stuck my hands through the top of the open sunroof, screaming, "Wait a minute, guys—I got my hands out the roof!"

When everything calmed down we told them we were Cowboys. They apologized, explaining to us what the street was known for. At first, they said, with that big car of ours and as slow as we were driving, they thought we might be pimps protecting our turf.

Except for that scary night, my first summer in Dallas was mellow. With the team coming off a 1–15 season, with people in Dallas still down on Jimmy and Jerry, there wasn't the Cowboy fever there is today. Though a few people recognized me—"Hey, there's the Cowboys' first-round draft pick"—I could usually cruise around without being noticed. I really enjoyed that, too. Even though I appreciate our fans, I have never been addicted to the spotlight. Other people might, but I certainly never think of myself as famous. I'm just a man who happens to play pro football.

■ ■ ■

When training camp began in mid-July, I still had no contract with the Cowboys. They were offering $3.2 million for five years. I wanted something shorter, so I could prove myself in the NFL, then go back to the table to get my real value. So I wanted two years at $3.2 million. Which meant we weren't even close.

While the Cowboys convened at our camp in Austin, Texas, I returned to Pensacola. I saw no reason to stay nearby. The Cowboys had made it clear they would take their sweet time.

In the course of negotiations, the Cowboys were doing what's commonly known as slotting. Because I had lasted until the seventeenth pick, that's how they wanted to pay me. But Jerry Jones had already said it on the radio: The Cowboys had me rated fourth in the whole draft. If they were going to slot me, I felt they should slot me fourth, or at least much closer to fourth than seventeenth. I didn't feel this was outrageous, or even unreasonable. The number "four" was based on reality. After all the time and effort the Cowboys put into this draft, that's where they ranked me. The number "seventeen" was based largely on circumstance: Most teams went for defense in that year's first round. Among offensive players, only Jeff George, Blair Thomas, Andre Ware, and Richmond Webb were drafted before me.

During our impasse, Jerry Jones took some shots in the

press at my agent, Richard Howell. Among the several agents who contacted me, I had decided on Richard for several reasons. His client list wasn't huge, so I felt he'd give me the concentration I needed. He didn't represent any big-name football players, but in basketball he had two major talents: Mark Price of the Cavaliers and Georgia Tech coach Bobby Cremins. I also liked Richard personally, but most important to me I felt I could trust him. I could never see Richard selling me out, making a bad deal for me so he could suck up to the Cowboys. As obnoxious as that sounds, it's exactly what some agents do.

That summer, Jerry Jones made Richard Howell seem like the bad guy. Jerry called him a "holdout agent." He implied he'd never draft another of Richard's clients. Though Jerry did not attack me, I felt his statements about Richard were uncalled for. Richard was only doing what any good agent does: He was fighting for his client. Furthermore, Jerry was making our stalemate look one-sided, when everyone knows it takes two to reach an agreement.

Unfortunately, by late August, with the regular season just two weeks away, Richard had no real progress he could report. So with Florida about to start its fall semester, I drove down to Gainesville and enrolled. If I couldn't play football that year, I planned on earning more credits toward my degree. When the news hit that I was enrolling in college, some people called it a negotiating ploy. It wasn't. It also wasn't a bluff. It was my parents' idea. They saw how things were going with the Cowboys. When I could be in school, why sit home and wait for something that might not materialize?

It was great advice. Once I got back on campus I felt

THE EMMITT ZONE

more relaxed. I still thought about playing football, but it became secondary to going to school. I told Richard Howell to call me with something concrete; otherwise he could handle this without me.

We finally made a deal September 4, five days before our first game, against San Diego. As I said, the Cowboys had started at five years for $3.2 million. We wanted two years at $3.2 million. We settled on three years at about $3 million. Included in that was about a $1 million signing bonus.

The day after I signed, I couldn't help shaking my head when I read about the deal in the newspapers. The Cowboys were saying my contract was for four years. Why? Because that's how they dressed it up. But in effect, that fourth year was nullified the moment I played my first down. Evidently, the Cowboys didn't bother telling the press that.

I knew why the Cowboys did it—to try to save some face—and I didn't care. So I didn't even bother correcting the media. Later that season, I did tell Dallas reporters, for no particular reason: "Hey, guys, my contract is actually for three years. The fourth year was wiped out when I stepped on the football field." The reporters checked it out and saw it was true. They've called it a three-year deal ever since.

I didn't care what the Cowboys were telling the press—I had a signing-bonus check for $1 million! When I first took it home, I literally ran shouting around my apartment. Then I got right on the phone with my mom. Later my rookie season, I helped my parents remodel their home. I also bought my father a Corvette. I'd always known it was his dream car.

And this was the nicest part about suddenly having this money: I could do things for the people who helped me the most.

9
HELLO,
NFL

Some rookies come into this league like they're everything and all that.

I wasn't one of those rookies. Only twenty-one years old, and also a first-round pick who had missed all of training camp, I wanted to stay in the background and not ruffle any egos. So I came in reserved. I spoke to my teammates, of course, but I didn't elaborate much except with my fellow runners. Three of them in particular—Keith Jones, Tommie Agee, and Daryl Johnston—were especially helpful to me in learning the system.

While I didn't come in with my mouth working overtime, I did have some big-time goals. I wanted to lead the NFL in rushing, be named Rookie of the Year and Most Valuable Player, and help our team to win the Super Bowl. On a more pragmatic level, I hoped to help in establishing the Cowboys' running game, and in taking some of the pressure off Troy Aikman. In 1989, Troy's rookie year, Dallas had a revolving door for a roster, the running game never jelled, and he took a physical beating. One year later, I felt I could be the guy to give him that extra two seconds, so Troy could have time to pass the ball downfield.

Joe Brodsky, at first, didn't see it that way. Our hard-nosed backfield coach, Joe's a guy who enjoys blowing your mind. He talks tough and he talks nonstop, so he can keep you off balance. When I finally joined the Cowboys, the first thing out of Joe's mouth was "You ain't in shape to play football."

But I thought I was. And when I didn't start our first game against the Chargers, I felt disappointed. The Cowboys told the press I wasn't quite ready, I still had to learn the system, but I knew our entire game plan cold. It was the same exact stuff we worked on at quarterback school all summer. That didn't seem to matter to our coaches. In my first game as a pro, I carried twice for 2 yards.

I was not about to complain to Jimmy Johnson. As I mentioned before, the man was tightly wound my rookie year. Even with the season already started, Jimmy was constantly signing new players every day, cutting other ones on the spot, telling one guy with asthma to get his ass up off the practice field.

By the second game of the season, against the Giants, I

EMMITT SMITH

Celebrating the first touchdown of Super Bowl XXVIII with my teammates.

(RON ST. ANGELO)

With my brother, Erik
(*left*), in 1973.
(COURTESY OF
THE SMITH FAMILY)

Playing for the
Pop Warner Football
League in seventh
grade; I was eleven.
(COURTESY OF
THE SMITH FAMILY)

The 1989 homecoming game at Florida Field.

(STEPHEN MORTON)

At Florida, breaking free for a first down.

(COURTESY OF THE UNIVERSITY OF FLORIDA)

Breaking to the end zone against Buffalo in my second Super Bowl.

(*Above left and below*) Stretching and getting my game face on before meeting the Phoenix Cardinals.

With Hall of Fame running back Tony Dorsett, the Cowboys' current all-time leading runner, at my twenty-fifth birthday party earlier this year.

(SYLVIA DUNNAVANT)

Michael Irvin and I at the Dallas Cowboys' practice facility last year.

(SYLVIA DUNNAVANT)

My family: my brothers (*left to right*) Emil, Emory, and Erik; me;
my mother and father, Emmitt II and Mary; and my sister, Marsha.

(CAROL MCINTOSH)

A 1993 *Monday Night Football* game against the Philadelphia Eagles.

(RON ST. ANGELO)

Taking a handoff from Troy and following the "Moose" Daryl Johnston against the Bills in my first Super Bowl.

(RON ST. ANGELO)

was starting at tailback. And immediately I could see how serious pro ball was. The players swarmed to the ball much faster than those in college, and once they arrived they brought a heavier load. This was also the game when L.T. punched me in the face, and while it's funny now it hurt like hell at the time. Considering how excited I had been, my first NFL start turned into a downer. The Giants won 28–7, and I carried only 6 times.

Six carries? I couldn't believe it. I wanted to feel like I was part of our offense. I wanted to earn my money.

It was more of the same the next two weeks. As I averaged just 14 carries, we lost two more games in our conference. Next up was Tampa Bay at Texas Stadium. With our record at 1–3, our coaching staff felt it was time to change our tactics. They told me during our meetings all that week: "Okay, Emmitt, you're getting the football this Sunday."

Our coaches kept their word. On 23 carries, I had 121 yards and my first big day as a pro as we defeated Tampa Bay 14–10. But the following week I was back down to 12 carries. The Cardinals beat us in Phoenix, 20–3, and our offense looked horrible all afternoon. Everyone's frustration was starting to show, including offensive coordinator David Shula's. In the press conference after the game, he pointed the finger at me for blowing a crucial play. The only thing is, I didn't blow it.

Coach Shula was asked about our anemic showing. He said we had had some breakdowns, that some players had made mental errors. Then one writer wanted to know about one of Troy's interceptions. My job on that play was to block at the side of our tackle. I was told to stay tight, so no one could get between us. If a defensive player tried running to my outside, I was supposed to let him go. This was a bang-bang play: Troy would have gotten rid of the ball by then.

I followed our procedure against the Cardinals. I sealed off the end of our tackle's butt, and I let the defensive player swing around wide. But for some reason Troy never got the pass off. The guy on the Cardinals hit him just as he tried to, the ball flew up in the air, and it was picked off.

That play killed a drive that might have got us back into it. When the media asked Coach Shula what had happened, he said the mistake was mine. He said I missed my block.

Standing nearby, I got irate. Even if I had missed my block, I thought it was wrong for a coach to single out players that way.

A few minutes later, I was still steaming when I went up to take questions. Before we even got started, I asked the reporters how many carries I had. Someone said, "Twelve." I asked what I'd averaged on those 12 carries. The same guy said, "Four yards a carry."

I told the reporters, "Well, if a man is averaging four yards a carry, maybe they should give him the ball more often. I don't see why they keep passing the ball so much. They should be running the ball more often."

Some players make statements like this and reporters don't even bother writing it down. But since I wasn't known as a guy who had a big mouth, it turned into pretty big news when it made the papers. And even though I was mad at the time I said it, this was something that had been building up all season. Every week we'd gone into offensive meetings, and every week the offensive coaches had said: "We need to rush for one hundred yards in order to beat this team. Let's make this a team goal." Then Sunday would come and we'd abandon our plan. Each time it happened I got more perturbed. Coach Shula's comment in Phoenix just pushed me over the line.

To his credit, he didn't seem to hold any grudge against me. And except for being too rigid, Coach Shula seemed to me like a nice enough guy. Then again, I made it a point to get along with him. If an offensive coordinator dislikes a running back, he might keep the football away from him.

Though I never felt Coach Shula did that to me, I don't believe he recognized my talent. I also don't think that the running game was his strength. Coach Shula came to Dallas straight from Miami, where he had worked as one of his father's assistants. With Dan Marino and all those great receivers, the passing game excelled there. But the ground game was not exactly flourishing.

After our loss to the Cardinals, I still carried just 16 times against Tampa Bay. We beat them anyway, to put us at 3–4. With the Eagles, Jets, and 49ers next, this was a critical stretch if we hoped to make the playoffs. But in those next three games, I averaged 11 carries and we lost them all. Over the last two, our offense did not score a touchdown.

This included our 24–6 loss to San Francisco. My line that day was 6 carries for 40 yards, for a 6.7-yard average per carry. As a group, our running backs carried 15 times for 78 yards, a 5.2-yard average. San Francisco hadn't stopped us on the ground. We had stopped ourselves.

Nothing had changed since I spoke out in Phoenix. Meanwhile, we lost three big games to plummet to 3–7.

Thinking enough is enough, this time I went to back-field coach Joe Brodsky. "Coach," I said, "I'm still hearing the same things I've heard all year: 'We need to gain a hundred yards on the ground.' You told us that again before we played San Francisco. Then you give the running backs fifteen carries. That's too much pressure on Troy, and it's not enough work for us."

Joe, for once, didn't say much. He knew I was upset, and I wanted him to know. Maybe this way he'd talk to David Shula. Even though Jimmy Johnson was our head coach, it was David's job to call our offensive plays.

Somebody must have taken my input to heart. That Sunday against the Rams I carried 21 times. Though I gained only 54 yards, all those carries kept the defense from cheating up against Troy. He threw for 3 touchdowns that game, Michael Irvin had 2 TDs and 71 yards receiving, and we beat the Rams in Anaheim, 24–21.

As our entire offense came back to life, I also caught 4 passes that game, for 117 yards. Man, did I love that. I'm not just a runner, you know. I can catch the ball too.

Most people didn't know this when I was at Florida. With our offense always in flux, I caught only 56 passes in three college seasons. But I always felt I had the skills to catch more, and I proved it once I got to the NFL. In my four years as a pro, I've caught 24, 49, 59, and 57 passes. And as many running backs move from college to pro, you see this happen a lot. His entire career at Jackson State, Walter Payton caught 27 passes; in his NFL career, Walter caught 422.

I take my pass-receiving very seriously. It diversifies our passing game, so other teams can't just key on our wide receivers. It gives me more chances to break some tackles, maybe turn a small play into a long one. It also means my game is more complete. I never want to be known as a one-dimensional back. I'd rather emulate people like Walter Payton or, in today's game, Thurman Thomas and Marcus Allen. Like Walter Payton, Marcus and Thurman can run, catch passes, *and* block.

It's hard to say exactly why some backs are better receivers than others. Like running with the ball, I think a lot of it is instinct; you're either a natural receiver or you're not. Having good concentration is also important. So is having good hands. But I'll tell you one thing that often gets overlooked: whether or not a guy can run disciplined routes. I mean this for all receivers, not just running backs. Because no matter how fast or tough a receiver is, a sloppy route will usually kill a pass play. That's why, on most teams, you'll find at least one receiver who doesn't have that much speed, or that many moves, but who runs his routes as if he's cleaning his watch. These are the detail guys, the guys a quarterback knows he can depend on.

■　■　■

Our game after the Rams was big in several respects. With our record at 4–7, we still had an outside chance of making it into the playoffs. Our four wins also meant that we had improved on the Cowboys' last two seasons of 1–15 and 3–13. Now people around the league were looking harder at us. Were the Dallas Cowboys really on their way back, or were they still a troubled franchise?

That Thursday in Dallas against the Redskins, we sent a message to the rest of the NFL. In a national TV game on Thanksgiving, we fell behind 17–10 about midway through the third quarter. It didn't look good for us, either. After intercepting Troy, the Redskins had the ball and the momentum. But rather than lose our resolve, we just kept fighting. And from midway through the third quarter until the final gun, we scored 17 unanswered points to win 27–17.

This was a pivotal day for our entire offense. Twenty-seven points was more than we'd scored in one game all year, and it came against a respected Washington defense. With a few of our offensive linemen still learning new positions, they were finally starting to feel like they were a unit. Troy Aikman's back was aching that afternoon, but he still played great when it counted most, hitting 9 of 10 passes late in the game. Afterwards, when asked about his hot streak, Troy said, "It was probably the best I've ever played in this league."

My own performance was also a confidence booster. In my biggest game as a rookie, I gained 132 yards and scored 2 touchdowns. On my second TD, in the fourth quarter, I went off right guard, cut sharply to the left, and broke it for 48 yards. This was important to me, for two reasons: It helped close out the Redskins, and I stiff-armed Darrell Green on my way to the end zone. Darrell's one of the finest corners who has ever played the game.

After we beat the Redskins on national television, I

EMMITT SMITH

could have floated off the football field. But normally I don't like playing games on Thanksgiving. After playing the Sunday before, my body is still in shock when that Thursday comes. I suck it up, like everyone else, but it isn't easy. With the soreness I always feel after a game, the body parts out of alignment, I can feel battered for weeks after we play. Toward the end of the season, there are very few parts of my body that *don't* feel damaged.

I really don't think the average fan understands this. They see the network graphics and colorful uniforms—for them it's all rah-rah-rah and win win win. That's only one part of professional football, though. Beneath the glamour this sport is intensely violent. Football players just keep getting bigger and faster, and when two guys collide out there it sounds like a car wreck. And the fans never see us *after* the game. They never come into our training room, where we bleed and ache and swell. That's nobody's fault, of course. It's just something I think the fans should be aware of. This game has large rewards, but also high prices.

That's why people should not take it wrong when they see me after a game. If they pat me on my shoulder or on my back, and I cringe or wince, it has nothing to do with them. I appreciate the gesture, but how about just walking up and shaking my hand? With as many hits as I take to my shoulder and back, they might be sore at the moment.

■ ■ ■

After our offensive surge against the Redskins, we came back to earth against all those hostile linebackers on the Saints, but we still managed to beat them, 17–14. Then, on December 16, we had our second meeting that year against

THE EMMITT ZONE

the Cardinals. Nine weeks earlier, at Sun Devil Stadium, their defense kicked our butts and we lost 20–3. This time, in Texas Stadium, we slaughtered them, 41–10. The Troy-and-Michael combo had more big plays, and our offensive line was devastating. Running behind them 24 times, I scored a career-high 4 touchdowns. On one TD run, from 11 yards out, I took a draw up the middle, cut and cut back, and shaked and baked into the end zone. As one national columnist described it, "He eluded six tackles, ducking and weaving all the way. . . . It was easily the most spectacular run at Texas Stadium this season."

See? Who says I can't run pretty?

Since my 24 carries were also a new career high, one reporter asked me after the game: "How many times do you *want* to carry the ball?"

"Every time," I said. "I want the ball in my hands on every play."

Then I added: "Be sure to put in there I was smiling when I said that."

I wasn't smiling that night—I was in pain. On one short-yardage play during the game, I'd tried flying over the top, and my right hand had gotten smashed between two Cardinal helmets. I never sat down, but it hurt severely and I thought I'd have trouble later. After the game, I did. So much blood and fluid had rushed into my finger, our doctor drilled a hole straight through my fingernail. It was the only way to release the pressure, he said.

With four straight wins and a record of 7–7, we had clawed our way back into wild-card contention. But in Philadelphia two days before Christmas, the Eagles had something we couldn't handle: their overpowering, gang-tackling, bad-attitudinal, headache-dispensing defense. That season the Eagles had Reggie White, Jerome Brown, Clyde Simmons, Seth Joyner, Byron Evans, Mike Golic, Eric Allen, Andre Waters, and Wes Hopkins.

Ouch. That's running back hell.

Quarterbacks weren't safe either. Before the first quarter was even ended that game, the Eagles had knocked out Troy with a separated shoulder. *With* Troy in the lineup it's hard beating Philadelphia; with a rusty Babe Laufenberg filling in, we lost 17–3. The strange thing about it was, Babe hardly played all season, yet he still threw 38 passes in less than four quarters. At the same time I dropped back down to 14 carries, even though my average that game was 4.4 yards per carry.

So once again I wasn't thrilled, and neither were our offensive linemen. Generally speaking, offensive linemen will always prefer to block for the run than the pass. On running plays, they get to fire out and attack the defensive player. On pass plays they're backing up, so they have to rely on their footwork and their finesse. And while they're trying to be so patient and controlled, those defensive linemen rush in like kamikazes. To counter that intensity, an offensive linemen must stand there and keep his cool. This takes tremendous restraint when a guy like Reggie White is bashing on you.

But much more important than any of that to our linemen, they want to win. And with Troy going down early against the Eagles, they all felt running the ball gave us our best chance. I recall thinking to myself after the game:

THE EMMITT ZONE

What just happened out there? With a backup quarterback playing, why ignore the ground game? Even if Troy had not gotten hurt, I couldn't see him throwing 38 times.

In our regular-season finale, we played at Atlanta, with Troy still out of commission. The Falcons were always blitz-happy to begin with, and that final Sunday they came at us in waves. It was terrible, just like the Auburn game when I was in college. Stacked up to stop the run, on some plays the Falcons blitzed ten guys. They blitzed everyone on their squad but Jerry Glanville.

I carried 16 times for 34 yards, a horrendous average of 2.1 yards per carry. The Falcons won 26–7, killing our hopes of slipping into the playoffs.

Though we finished only 7–9, this was six games better than the year before, and Jimmy Johnson won NFL Coach of the Year. I also won a few postseason awards, as the Associated Press and several more organizations named me their NFL Offensive Rookie of the Year. This was gratifying to me, because Rookie of the Year was one of my preseason goals.

What I didn't achieve that season was 1,000 yards. With 937, tops among rookies and tenth in the NFL, I still had a decent first year. But it didn't satisfy me. One thousand yards was another rookie goal, and I felt I should have reached it. But with 241 carries that season, an average of only 15 a game, I didn't.

I wasn't alone. Our entire offense felt frustrated that year. For all the talent we had, our coaching staff never utilized all our weapons. And when the NFL posted its final statistics, we ranked 28th and last in offensive production.

EMMITT SMITH

In six of our nine losses, we scored 7, 3, 9, 6, 3, and 7 points.

Jimmy Johnson couldn't sit still on something like this, and after the season he made two difficult choices. First he demoted David Shula, whom Jimmy had great respect for. Then, to replace him, Jimmy hired a relative unknown. But Jimmy had found the perfect man for the job. His name was Norv Turner.

10
NEW DAY
IN DALLAS

By the summer of 1991, all signs pointed to a revitalized Cowboy offense.

Michael Irvin, at full strength again after knee surgery sidelined him our first four games last season, was a superstar ready to happen.

In that spring's NFL draft, seeking another big-play receiver, the Cowboys took Alvin Harper in the first round. He was the twelfth player picked, unusually high for a wide receiver, but Jimmy Johnson felt Alvin was somebody special. Alvin also came from Tennessee, a school known for producing high-powered receivers.

Jay Novacek, our sure-handed, clutch, deceptively quick

tight end, was coming off the best season of his career. In 1990, Jay had led all tight ends with 59 pass receptions.

Troy Aikman, his shoulder healed, was back to throw to them all.

Backing up Troy was a rock-solid Steve Beuerlein, whom we'd just picked up in a key trade with the Raiders.

Lining up directly behind our quarterbacks, we had our fullback, Daryl "Moose" Johnston. Nobody's tougher than Moose, nobody works any harder, and no one appreciates him more than I do. Moose has his own thing going on. He's one of those rare backs who can run, block, and catch passes, and at 238 pounds he does it all with great force. But Moose does something else: He sells his body for me. Week after week, he sticks his head in the tightest holes, and blasts them open. I really don't know where I'd be without the guy. Moose allows me to be the pro runner I'd always hoped to be.

Speaking of tough guys, I can't forget the big hosses up front that year: Nate Newton, Mark Tuinei, Kevin Gogan, Mark Stepnoski, John Gesek, Frank Cornish, and our ferocious rookie, Erik Williams. Going into that season, they weren't getting the ink that our other players were, but even that would come. They were quickly earning a place among the league's elite units.

I was ready to rumble that season too. With one year of experience behind me, I set my goals even higher than the previous year. I wanted to lead the NFL in rushing, run for 1,500 to 2,000 yards, improve from 24 catches to 30 or 40, and then be named league MVP.

I wasn't kidding myself. With Norv Turner running our offense, I felt anything was possible that season.

EMMITT SMITH

The first time I met him, that summer, he was sitting by the pool at my apartment complex. I didn't know it was Norv, and I didn't know he'd just moved there. After one of my teammates pointed him out, I walked up to him and we made our introductions. Norv seemed totally open-minded and unpretentious, so I cut right to the chase.

I said, "What's the game plan this season, Coach? You gonna get me the football, or what?"

We both started laughing, then talked about our new system. Norv said it would be easy for us to pick up, and that's exactly what happened. Norv believed in a limited number of plays, executed precisely again and again. That sounded perfect to me, especially since we played in the NFC East. Against teams like the Giants, Redskins, Eagles, and Cardinals, you don't win with tricky plays; you win with sound, relentless, physical football.

I was also pleased when I heard about Norv's background. Because he had played quarterback in college, some people said Norv would come in doing nothing but passing. Norv *did* know the passing game, and he was eager to work with Troy Aikman. But Norv had also coached at USC, a mother lode of great runners, and later with the Rams, when Eric Dickerson played there. Though never a running back coach, Norv had learned to appreciate their skill and their art.

But even as optimistic as everyone felt about Norv, this was still Jimmy's team, and he wasn't exactly shrinking into the background. Before my rookie year, even though his last team had just gone 1–15, Jimmy had told the press: "I expect us to win as many as we lose." We only went 7–9, but Troy was injured our last two games, and Jimmy was

THE EMMITT ZONE

not about to start censoring himself. Before our next season he said, "Not only will we make the playoffs, but we will have success in the playoffs."

Remarks like that don't win humility contests. But Jimmy has this credo: If you can walk the walk, you're allowed to talk the talk. I had my own saying: Jimmy Johnson was good at writing checks, but it was up to our players to go out and cash them. (And, actually, Jerry writes the checks!)

I say that with a chuckle, which is how I always reacted to Jimmy's announcements. Even when Jimmy predicted a win before a particular game, I never felt he was putting more pressure on us. Games are won and lost on Sundays, out on the field, not during the week in the newspapers.

Before I do run out there every Sunday, first I have to go through my pregame ritual. Though it's not about superstition, I must have the same routine every week. Nothing can vary. To perform at my best, I need a feeling of clarity and order.

Like most NFL teams, we stay in a hotel the night before every game, even when we play in Dallas. Some players don't care for this much, but I think it's a good idea. It keeps our guys off the street, off their feet, eating right and watching film and getting prepared for the game. Hanging out that night together, as a group, we also get a feeling of solidarity. And once the action begins, a football team can never be too close.

When I wake up on game day, I'm not one of those players who are already feeling ornery. On the contrary, I wake up happy. Happy about life. Happy that I play in the NFL.

EMMITT SMITH

Happy that I can compete. Even if I wake up and my *body* feels lousy, I instantly set my mind: Today will be a great day.

Some mornings, of course, feeling positive and upbeat is harder than others. Sometimes, for no reason I can explain, I wake up with something that feels like fear. Not fear of getting injured, but fear of not performing. I don't try denying this feeling when it comes. I also don't let it tie me in knots. I tell myself: This is nothing to be ashamed of. It's natural, in fact. It just shows how much I want to win and perform. Hey! I can take this edgy feeling and turn it to my advantage. I can let it drive me onto the football field. Then I can unleash my monsters on my opponents.

Most mornings I also wake up hungry, so I head straight downstairs to our pregame meal. But I don't want to feel even semi-lethargic, so I get some bacon and eggs, some waffles and orange juice, and then I don't eat it all. At kickoff time, I still want to feel some physical hunger.

Still at our hotel, we enter our offensive meeting, where Norv Turner reiterates our game plan and how we're going to run our two-minute drill. After the offense breaks into smaller groups, I attend our team chapel service. Not everyone goes, but a lot of guys do, and it's something I look forward to every week. Going to chapel soothes my nerves. It also lets me give thanks for the gifts that I have received.

Depending on what time the game is, then it's either back to our rooms or straight to the stadium. For a typical Sunday game at 1 P.M., I arrive in our locker room around 10:30. I head straight for my locker, put my bag of CDs in,

walk over to the chalkboard, and sign up to be taped by our
trainer, Kevin O'Neill. I like to be taped and partially
dressed before too many guys get there, so I can hang out
alone in front of my locker, alone with my music, alone in
my own private space.

I listen to rap music first, maybe Snoop Doggy Dogg or
Ice Cube. Then I like to ease back down as game time closes
in, so I'll put on some slower music, maybe something in-
strumental like Enigma. After stretching on my own for
about twenty minutes, I stretch again with our strength
coach, Mike Woicik. By now it's almost noon, time to jog
out on the field and stretch *again*, this time as a team in one
corner of the end zone. We do our segment work, and it's
back to the locker room just before kickoff. I grab my
mouthpiece, but don't put it in yet. We say our team prayer.
The referee comes in yelling, "Two minutes, two minutes."
Jimmy keeps his pep talk brief. The time for words has
passed, and Jimmy knows it. Now it's time for work.

■ ■ ■

With four straight NFC East teams coming up next, our
first game at Cleveland was even more important than
most season openers. And right out of the gate, Norv
Turner showed how much faith he had in our running
game. In a 26–24 win, I carried the ball a career-high 32
times. Combined with my 6 pass receptions, I handled the
ball 38 times. This was the busiest day for a Cowboy runner ever, breaking the old mark of 36 held by Herschel
Walker and Calvin Hill.

In any NFL game, let alone the first one, that's a lot of

work for a running back. But I never expected the media flurry it started. In his game story on Monday, Dan Noxen of the *Dallas Morning News* said, "Overall, Smith hit the rock-hard Cleveland Stadium surface nearly 50 times." Then the call-in radio shows jumped into the debate, questioning whether the Cowboys would burn me out. Reacting to that, Skip Bayless headlined his Wednesday *Dallas Times Herald* column: "Don't worry—Emmitt can carry a heavy load." On Friday, responding to Bayless, Blackie Sherrod headlined his own *Dallas Morning News* column: "Emmitt carry the full load? Balderdash!"

The media and fans were more whipped up than I was. If I carried 32 times week after week, then, yes, I would feel my longevity was at risk. But it was only our first game, our offense had the football most of the day, and we needed this win badly with four NFC East games coming up next. As for the bigger picture, I also knew the NFL has no guarantees. A long career is something I would love, but it isn't promised to me or anyone else. So until my last day comes, I'll just keep on running.

When I woke up that Monday morning, I had so many welts and abrasions it hurt just to take a shower. It was more than the frozen ground Dan Noxen had written about—the Browns had hit ferociously that game. On one goal-line play, two of them slammed their helmets into mine, and I actually thought I heard ringing inside my brain. On another play, I got gang-tackled by six or seven guys. Lying facedown on the field, trying to keep the Browns from knowing they hurt me, I rolled over and saw Mike Irvin standing over me.

"You all right?" Mike said.

When I saw that no Browns were around, I told him, "No! These boys are sticking me, man!"

In our next game, a 33–31 loss at home to Washington, I didn't need any help from the other team; I did something terrible to myself.

In our game against the Browns, my legs had begun feeling numb in the second half. It was nothing serious, just fatigue. When I mentioned this on the sideline to Daryl Johnston, he said, "I have some stuff for you, Emmitt. You can try it next week. It will give you some extra energy."

Before the Washington game, Moose showed me his powdered food supplement in our locker room. I don't even remember what it was called, but I guess it was designed to give you potassium. Anyway, Moose mixed some in water, and it looked horrible. I hesitated to drink it, but Moose said, "You may want to do it right now. This stuff might sit on your stomach."

I downed it. It tasted worse than it looked. And it sat on my stomach, all right. Like a bowling ball.

It was only September 9, still hot and humid in Dallas, and even before the kickoff I felt weak and clammy. Then, in the first quarter, I broke a 75-yard touchdown run. Guys were hugging and pounding on me, and honest to goodness I thought I was going to yack. Then I *did* yack, right on the sideline after that run. I was yacking that energy drink all over. I felt so light-headed and dizzy when I was through, I thought I might float off the field and into the stands.

By halftime I was dehydrated so badly, they had to stick

an IV in my arm. I felt stronger after that, but my stomach was still cramping up when the third quarter started. In the first half, I had carried 9 times for 109 yards; in the second half, I carried twice for 3 yards. Obviously, I wasn't much help as the Redskins beat us 33–31. And at one point I told Moose: "I'm never drinking that stuff anymore!"

By 1991, not counting games played during the NFL strike, the Eagles had beaten the Cowboys eight times in a row. On Sunday they made it nine, squashing us 24–0. Bad enough that it happened at home, but this made us 0–2 in the NFC East.

One week later we got our first conference win, beating the Cardinals 17–9 in Phoenix. On just our third play from scrimmage, I took a handoff up the middle, found a seam, and dashed for a 60-yard touchdown. In our last two games, I now had touchdown runs of 60 and 75 yards. From that point on in my second year, I rarely heard anyone question my "breakaway speed."

I ended up the game with 182 yards, my new single-game high. With 450 yards after four weeks, this also put me on top of the NFL rushing charts. I'd never been there before, and all that week in Dallas the newspaper stories were asking: Could Emmitt be the Cowboys' first rushing king? It was surprising, but true. With all the exceptional runners who'd played in Dallas—Don Perkins, Duane Thomas, Calvin Hill, Robert Newhouse, and Herschel Walker—none had ever led the NFL in rushing.

Even Tony Dorsett had never done it. The most prolific Cowboy runner of all time, he was also the fourth-leading rusher in NFL history. So I suppose it was inevitable: That

THE EMMITT ZONE

first Sunday when I took the rushing lead, the media started comparing us again. This had begun my rookie year, almost from my first big game, and it always left me with mixed emotions. Flattered to even be mentioned with Tony Dorsett, I also got tired of people defining my game by how it related to Tony's. I'm sure Tony felt the same way. Because everyone who plays running back has his own style, and that style comes out of his own unique personality. So even though it's no big deal, most runners don't really enjoy it when people lump us together. We'd all like to be seen as individuals.

■　■　■

Our victory over the Cardinals ignited a hot streak. In the next three weeks, we knocked off the defending Super Bowl champion Giants, the Green Bay Packers, and the Cincinnati Bengals. After a loss to Detroit put us at 5–3, the Cardinals made their yearly visit to Texas Stadium. And I did something I never do: I didn't give our opponents their due respect.

In our first game against the Cardinals that season, I had gained 182 yards. In week thirteen of my rookie year, I'd scored 4 touchdowns against them. Even though we won this game 27–7, I came into it mentally unprepared— and the Cardinals made me pay. In holding me to 62 yards on 22 carries, they also put some nasty licks on me. One play while I was running down the sideline, a Cardinal stuck his helmet into my groin. The pain was excruciating—and I had it coming. So I had a few big games against the Cardinals; I was still way out of line to take them lightly.

EMMITT SMITH

On November 10, in the Astrodome, things didn't get any better. In fact, I'd never felt lower in my career.

In our desire to make the playoffs, the Houston game marked the start of another important stretch. With two more road games following this one, a win would put us at 7–3. A loss would mean 6–4, with always-hard games in New York and Washington next.

The Oilers always tend to play the Cowboys tough, and I felt frustrated this game from the beginning. The Oilers were stuffing me everywhere I went. It was just one of those days where I couldn't make anything happen.

The game went into overtime. It was still 23–23, with six minutes left, when I got the football and finally saw some daylight. After struggling all game, I wanted to win it for us.

But I ran into the back of Michael Irvin, who was blocking downfield for me. The football squirted loose and Houston recovered. As I stood on the sideline feeling sick, Warren Moon drove them down to the other end of the field, where they kicked a field goal to win 26–23.

Nobody was madder at me than I was. The Oilers recovered that ball at their own 17. Meaning that we were already in field goal range. Meaning I should have gone down, instead of trying to be everyone's hero. I'm a professional runner. There was no excuse on earth for what I did. To make me feel even worse, we had actually talked about this during the week. In making one of his uncanny predictions, Jimmy Johnson had told us: "I think this game will be tight. I want every point we can get. If we're already in field goal range, I want you guys down on the ground. Don't get any more yards than you need."

THE EMMITT ZONE

Inside our locker room after the game, I didn't talk to a soul. I didn't say: "This one was my fault." My teammates already knew I felt that way.

Michael Irvin saw me hurting and walked over. He said, "Don't worry about it, champ. You've won more games than you'll ever lose for us."

I also talked to my mom after the game. She said, "Baby, let it go. Shake it off and go get 'em next week."

I honestly tried to. Back in Dallas that Sunday night, I even went as planned to a Luther Vandross concert. But I couldn't loosen up enough to enjoy it. In the VCR inside my head, I kept rewinding my fumble. It was the only thing I could see.

I was so wired that night I could barely stay in my bed. On Monday morning I did some self-appraisal: I blew it yesterday. Badly. The entire city of Dallas is probably talking about it. But where do I go from here? Do I hang my head all week? Or do I try to do what my mother advised, just deal with the fact and keep on moving ahead?

That's what I desperately wanted to do. But rather than redemption, all I got in New York was more frustration.

It started with a bad call by the referees, a call the NFL would later reverse (but not until after the season, when it made no difference). For the most part, I think refs in the NFL do an excellent job. But in New York they botched it.

Though we lost 22–9, the game was still close when I swung out of the backfield and Troy threw me a short pass that slid through my hands, down my jersey, and onto the field. I made a lousy play, but I never had possession, so I just stood there watching the ball bounce. Lawrence Taylor

EMMITT SMITH

jumped on it, but I figured, So what? You can't recover an incomplete pass.

Then the doggone referee called it a reception and fumble. The Giants took over and quickly scored a touchdown.

Jimmy Johnson was on the refs the rest of the day. And later on in the game, with Jimmy disputing one crucial call after another, I fumbled for real. As I came off the field Jimmy was seething.

He said, "I don't know where your head is at today! But you damn better get it back here in this football game!"

Jimmy's outburst shocked me—and that was good. At twenty-two years old, I needed that wake-up call from Jimmy Johnson. It straightened me up for the rest of the year, and it couldn't have come at a better time. With our record at 6–5, our final five games would make or break us.

Our very next game, on November 24, was our biggest one of the season. At least on paper, it also figured to be our most difficult. On their way to winning that season's Super Bowl, the Redskins were 11–0. The game would also be played at RFK Stadium, where the fans are rowdy and close and Washington rarely loses.

In a very physical game between two longtime rivals, Washington led 7–0 after one quarter. But then, just as Jimmy told us he would all week, he began rolling the dice. Against such a powerful team on their home field, Jimmy said playing it safe wouldn't get it done; we needed to let it rip.

Our first gamble came in the second quarter, when we went for it on fourth down on Washington's 40 and made it. On our next series, still trailing 7–0, we had third and 15 at the Washington 32. Everyone in the stadium knew we'd be passing—which is why we ran a draw play. The Redskins were so surprised and our blocking was so crisp, I ran it all the way in for a 32-yard touchdown.

Cowboys 7, Redskins 7.

Just a few moments later, Jimmy fooled them again with an onside kick. When one of our players recovered, our sideline went crazy. Who even *tries* an onside kick in the second quarter?

When our offense ran back out, I couldn't wait to see linebacker Andre Collins. He'd been talking trash all game, telling me: "You ain't nothing! I'm gonna beat your butt all day!" I'd mostly kept my mouth shut, but not anymore. After my 32-yard TD run I told Andre: "Hey, where were you on my touchdown run? Huh? I didn't see you."

"I wasn't in the game that play," Andre said.

"That's right, man. You're not *good* enough to be in the game when I am."

This only irked him more, and Andre kept giving me noise. One time I told him, "Why don't you just shut your big mouth and play defense? *I'm* out here picking up four yards a carry, and *you're* running off at the mouth."

Some games, like this one, I can't help talking back to my opponents. But normally I just let my performance speak. I don't have time for distractions out there, and that's really what talking trash is all about: making you focus on them and not your assignment. But I wasn't born last week, and I also am not intimidated easily, so guys talking trash are pretty much wasting their breath.

I guess because Jimmy made all those bold statements

of his, some people felt our team talked more trash than any team in the league. I have no clue how to measure something like that. But I do know Alvin Harper was known to talk. On defense, I'm sure our guys had a steady rap going too. And then there was Michael Irvin.

Michael is more than just verbal by nature. He's the most competitive athlete I've ever met. Every week during practice, our two-minute drill is probably our most intense one. But nobody takes it more seriously than Michael. After he scores a TD on our defensive backs, he comes into our locker room screaming: "LARRY BROWN! KEVIN SMITH! COME HERE! TAKE MY SHOULDER PADS OFF! Now, when y'all take my shoulder pads off, I'm gonna take a shower! Larry, I want you to hang my shoulder pads up! Kevin, when I get outta the shower, I want you to dry me off! Because I own *both* of y'all! And whenever I tell you to get something done, I expect you to *do* it!"

It's all said with humor, and our players don't bat an eye. Michael is Michael.

Mentally and physically, Michael is also murder on our opponents. I've heard him tell young cornerbacks in this league: "Son, they keep y'all out here, they're gonna cut you tomorrow. I'm killing you, son. And I'm gonna kill you all day." One game he told a guy he'd just beaten deep: "It's a nightmare, isn't it? How can lightning keep striking like this?"

That's when he's getting the football. When he isn't, the volume gets cranked considerably. Hubbard Alexander is Michael's position coach; everyone calls him "Axe." When Michael feels slighted, he comes off the field shouting,

"AXE! AXE! AXE! You didn't give me the ball! I'm wide open! I'm dying out there, I'm telling ya! I need the ball! I'm WIDE OPEN!"

Again, none of this fazes us. Everyone on our offense wants the football. Michael just gets more animated about it.

I began getting close to Mike my rookie year, when we roomed on the road the latter part of the season. I liked him immediately. It was obvious to me that unlike some great athletes, he cared about other people besides himself. Because even back then, one year before his breakthrough season, Mike was out doing community work in Dallas. He was mostly working with youth groups, putting in the hours, without ever calling a press conference to announce it. When I saw that I thought: This guy is much more substantial than people realize.

I still feel that way. For all his ego and bluster, Michael may be our football team's hardest worker. He learned to work hard from his parents, who raised seventeen kids in a poor Fort Lauderdale neighborhood. In my opinion, it's his childhood that still drives Michael Irvin today. Or as Jimmy Johnson once said, "He's fought for food his whole life."

■ ■ ■

Back at RFK, Michael was doing a number on the Redskins. Despite being matched most plays against Darrell Green, he caught 9 passes for 130 yards and 1 touchdown. Alvin Harper made his presence known too. With time for only one last play in the first half, he made a great leaping catch of a Hail Mary pass into the end zone. Rather than being tied with the Redskins, it sent us into halftime leading 14–7. That's why Alvin Harper's nickname is "Highlight."

In the second half our defense took over, ending up with 5 sacks on their quarterback, Mark Rypien. With 132 yards on 34 carries, I also did my part. So did our backup quarterback, Steve Beuerlein, after Troy injured his knee in the second half. The moment Troy went down, I'm sure some people were writing off our season. But when Beuerlein entered our huddle, I didn't detect any panic on his part or ours. Instead he came in strong and self-assured. Before his first play he told us: "Okay, Troy is gone for now, but there's nothing to worry about. I'm running the show now. We're gonna keep this moving. Nothing is going to change."

It wasn't nervous chatter or false emotion. Beuerlein, above all, was real. And when he hit Mike for a 23-yard TD in the third quarter, we went on to give the Redskins their first loss that year. The final score was 24–21, but it wasn't that close; Washington scored a TD as time ran out.

The Thursday after that Sunday, we beat Pittsburgh on Thanskgiving to put us at 8–5. I ran the ball 32 times against the Steelers. With the 34 rushing attempts I had against the Redskins, that gave me 66 carries in only four days. In our next three games after that—against New Orleans, Philadelphia, and Atlanta—I rushed 27, 25, and 32 times. All told, I had 150 carries in our final five games that regular season. And that's when I felt concerned about my career. With Troy on the bench, I felt the Cowboys were telling me to carry our offense. The writers in Dallas noticed it too. And only because they brought it up first, I made a statement that December.

THE EMMITT ZONE

I said, "I don't have time to think about this now; we're in the midst of the season. So I'll keep doing what it takes to help us win ball games. But I'm sure this many carries, week after week, will have an effect in the future. And I want Jerry Jones to think about this when it comes time to do my next contract. Jerry talks about what it takes to win. He says we all need to sacrifice for the team. I think I've proven that I am willing to do that."

I wasn't saying I didn't want the football. I just wanted them to let Beuerlein do some more passing. That way I'd have my legs when the playoffs came, and I also thought we could win with Beuerlein passing. Next to Troy, he threw the long ball as well as any passer I'd seen. Outgoing and scrappy, Beuerlein was also a natural leader, while Troy at this time was hard to get to know. Today, Troy has changed, in my opinion. Much more relaxed and open, his personality is really starting to blossom.

With Beuerlein filling in, we closed out the regular season with five straight wins. In a critical game on December 15, we even beat the Eagles in Philadelphia. Going into this game, Jimmy Johnson was doing what he does best: making adjustments depending on our opponent. Against the unbeaten Redskins, Jimmy had gone for broke with onside kicks and Hail Marys. This week Jimmy told us, "We don't want to turn the ball over against this team; we want to play field position with them. We're going to win with tough defense and special teams."

Randall Cunningham was injured, and our defense sacked Jeff Kemp seven times that Sunday. Kelvin Martin broke an 85-yard punt return. Defense and special teams—

Jimmy had called it beautifully. As for our 25–13 win, it wasn't pretty at all. But it clinched our spot in the playoffs, and also gave Jimmy his first win against the Eagles.

With Beuerlein's five-game winning streak, the playoffs coming up, and Troy's knee getting stronger, a "quarterback controversy" was already under way. But that was among the media and the fans. As for my teammates and myself, we had every confidence in Beuerlein; we hated to think where we'd be after Troy went down if we hadn't traded for him. But Troy was our man. It wasn't even an issue. Troy stood tough in the pocket. He came up clutch in big games. He could rifle the ball or throw it with touch. He gave us everything we needed at his position.

We finished the regular season against Atlanta at home. Though our playoff spot was locked up, I had something personal at stake. In order to win my first NFL rushing title, I needed to have a big game. And I'm not about to tell you I didn't care. I wanted it bad, not only for pride but also for my next contract. I love this game and I want to be the best. I also want to be paid like I'm the best. I consider that only fair. But sometimes, unfortunately, that's not how things work out.

I gained 160 yards against Atlanta, giving me 1,563 for the regular season. At age twenty-two, I had my first rushing title! And look at the two guys I edged: Barry Sanders and Thurman Thomas!

Barry Sanders amazes me. The man makes moves I can't even comprehend. One Sunday night, I was up late watching highlights on ESPN. Barry made so many cuts on one touchdown run, I leaped in the air and started screaming. Nobody stops—and starts back up—faster than Barry. And believe me, Barry isn't stopping for long. He's frozen for an instant, looking for his hole—then he's moving again while the tackler's grabbing for air.

Most runners excel in one area, maybe two. Thurman Thomas shines at everything. Inside the tackles, Thurman slashes through without any hesitation. He also has speed to turn the corner on sweeps. He catches long sideline passes, short passes in the flat, out passes for first downs, underneath passes in linebacker country, deep-over-the-middle passes between the safeties. On top of all that, he blocks.

People always ask me: Do I consider Thurman and Barry rivals? The answer is no. Their performances inspire me. I also like seeing them play, because it's fun. I grew up on pro football. Even though I'm part of it now, I'm still a fan of people like Thurman and Barry.

■　■　■

Ending up 11–5 in the regular season, we qualified for the playoffs as a wild card. After five consecutive losing seasons in Dallas, including Tom Landry's last two years, this marked the first playoff game of the Jimmy and Jerry Era. It was also my own debut in the postseason, and I went in believing the Cowboys could win it all. I really did. I thought we had all the tools.

Emotionally, we were a team on the rise that was hungry to prove itself. Statistically, we were coming into the playoffs on a roll. In our five straight wins to end the regular season, our offense had averaged about 26 points a game. In three of our last four games, our defense had allowed only 4 touchdowns. We were also the youngest team in the NFL, so our legs would probably be fresher than those of our older opponents. That can mean a lot in December and January, when the long NFL season is taking its toll.

Still, I wasn't a fool. I wasn't looking past the Chicago Bears, our first-round opponent at Soldier Field. Five years earlier, when I was in college, I'd watched their defense lead the Bears to a Super Bowl win. Their current unit was not quite that fierce, but they still had serious people to contend with. Mike Singletary was still roaming the middle. Richard Dent, Steve McMichael, and Refrigerator Perry still anchored their front line. At safety they had Mark Carrier, a buddy of mine, and already a force in his second year in the league.

The Bears, of course, were also coached by Mike Ditka. I had never met the man, so I wasn't any authority, but I did wonder sometimes about his people skills. During his press conferences, I saw Ditka criticizing Chicago players by name. Even if players claim they don't, I know for a fact they take these things to heart. If their coach does it enough, they may feel their only way to retaliate is also through the media. Then you have controversy, which doesn't always mean a team will stop winning. But when controversy is mixed with players losing their spirit, that can be deadly.

Like everyone else who saw it, I was amazed at what Ditka did to Jim Harbaugh. Harbaugh threw an interception and Ditka went berserk. A coach has a right to chew out a player, but right then and there, so blatantly on the sideline in front of the world? On the Cowboys we call that "fronting." Most people call it humiliation, and I don't see how it could have helped Harbaugh's performance.

Anyway, we opened the playoffs by beating the Bears and Ditka, 17–13. In twenty-seven playoff games, dating all the way back to 1932, Chicago had never allowed a runner to gain 100 yards. On a cool, overcast day and a muddy field, I became the first. On 26 carries I rushed for 105 yards. On one of those runs, my darkest nightmare came true: The Refrigerator fell on top of me. I was lying on the bottom of the pile, yelling, "Get up! GET UP OFF OF ME!" At least I thought I was yelling; with the Fridge on me, I'm not sure I made any noise.

On another play, I was running at my friend Mark Carrier when I got smashed from behind by another Bear. The blow knocked me into Mark and he staggered backwards and fell. Mark can really hit, and he seemed surprised that I knocked him backwards like that. Since he didn't seem to know, I wasn't about to tell him I had some help.

The real story that game was our swarming defense. Going into the fourth quarter, all the Bears had were two Kevin Butler field goals. After their offense scored its first touchdown to make our lead 17–13, and then were driving again to pull in front, our defense put together a brilliant goal-line stand. This foreshadowed good things for the Cowboys' future: We had four or five rookies out there on that goal-line stand.

From the Windy City we went to the Motor City, where our season came crashing down with a 38–6 loss to the Detroit Lions. I never saw this coming. In the regular season, the Lions had beaten us 34–10. But that was in week eight, our execution was poor, and I thought we were a much stronger ball club now. We were, but we still couldn't handle the Lions. They came out smoking and scoring and never stopped. All season long, including our first game against Detroit, our defense struggled with teams that played the run-and-shoot. We were also keying that day on Barry Sanders, and Erik Kramer just kept throwing his out routes. In one of the sharpest games of his career, Kramer first-downed us to death.

You can't blame our defense, though; our offense played just as poorly. We couldn't sustain a drive. We turned the ball over four times. With the Lions way ahead of us, I had only 15 carries for 80 yards. Steve Beuerlein even got yanked out of the game, as Jimmy brought in Troy for the first time since his knee injury in November. I didn't feel it had much influence either way, but I was surprised when Jimmy pulled Beuerlein so quickly. Even though our offense had started slowly, I thought the game was still in reach, and that Beuerlein still had everything under control. I guess Jimmy inserted Troy to try to spark us. But this was Detroit's day, not ours.

Three weeks later I flew to Hawaii for my second straight appearance in the Pro Bowl. As a rookie, I'd become the first Cowboy to play in the Pro Bowl since Jerry and Jimmy took over. But I was named as an alternate, only because Neal Anderson couldn't go. So my second year was more satisfying to me: This time I was voted in, by my peers.

THE EMMITT ZONE

Unlike my first trip, when I was the only Cowboy, I now had three teammates whom I could hang out with: Michael Irvin, Jay Novacek, and Troy Aikman. In the first of several electric seasons to come, Michael had 93 receptions for a league-leading 1,523 yards. For the second year in a row, Jay led all tight ends in receptions, with 59. Troy, before his knee injury in week twelve, was leading the NFC in passing yards and completions.

You've probably noticed that all four of our Pro Bowl selections came on offense. I give Norv Turner a lot of credit for that. In our first year under his play-calling and system, I led the NFL in rushing, Michael Irvin led the league in receiving yards, and our offense jumped from twenty-eighth and last in the NFL to ninth. I think that says it all about Norv's impact.

Michael Irvin stole the show in Hawaii, but not without fighting for it. Initially, Mike was upset that he wasn't getting the ball from Atlanta Falcons quarterback Chris Miller. Instead, the NFC coaches were featuring Jerry Rice. So before Michael's first Pro Bowl could just pass him by, he went off like a rocket on the sideline.

"Give me the ball!" he screamed. "I led the league in receiving! Y'all wanna win? GIMME THE FOOTBALL!"

Once Chris Miller did, Michael wound up with 8 receptions, 125 yards, 1 touchdown, and the Pro Bowl MVP. No one will ever call Michael Irvin shy. But, boy, can he play football.

11 RISING TOWARD THE TOP

wanted a raise that summer. And after leading the NFL in rushing and carries, after becoming the youngest player in NFL history to gain more than 1,500 yards, after my second straight appearance in the Pro Bowl, I felt I deserved one. Not counting the money I could earn in incentives, my base salary my third year would be about $465,000. By NFL standards, this made me a bargain.

So with one year left to go on my three-year contract, my agent, Richard Howell, called Jerry Jones in June. Richard told Jerry my contract was nearly up. We'd like to renegotiate, Richard said, and we'd like to do it now, to keep us from all going through what we had my rookie year.

Jerry told Richard: "We want to take care of the players who are unsigned. Once we get done with them, we'll take care of Emmitt."

With training camp approaching, we still had eight veteran players who hadn't signed new contracts. Seven of them were starters: Ken Norton, Tony Tolbert, Vinson Smith, James Washington, Jay Novacek, Michael Irvin, and Mark Stepnoski.

So I didn't argue when I heard what Jerry said. I didn't sit out training camp. I waited my turn. I showed my good faith. Once the other guys were signed, I truly believed that Jerry would call me in, then give me a contract extension that I could feel good with. Not only was I one of Jerry's key players, but the Cowboys were not exactly hurting for money. According to an article in *Newsweek*, the Cowboys would soon become "the most valuable sports property in the universe."

Still, I started suspecting trouble when the rest of us left for training camp in Austin and Michael Irvin was still holding out in Dallas. Working mostly against the best cornerback on each team, Mike had just led the NFL in receiving yards. With his mental toughness and zest for the game, he was also important to us emotionally. When I saw how Jerry was dealing with Mike, I was pretty sure Jerry would drag things out with me too.

■ ■ ■

The final week of June, I heard some shocking and terrible news: Jerome Brown had died in an automobile accident.

I'd first met Jerome when I was a senior in high school.

EMMITT SMITH

In Ohio to get an award, I was thrilled to see Jerome Brown on my elevator. He was already a pro, I'd just committed to Florida, and Jerome started to tease me about my decision. In college, Jerome had played for Jimmy at Miami. Jerome said the boys down there would whip my Florida butt.

He seemed like a friendly giant, gregarious and funny away from the game, and that's just what Jerome Brown turned out to be. Once I joined the Cowboys, I got friendly with him through two other former Hurricanes—Alonzo Highsmith and Michael Irvin. Later on, just four months before he died, I hung out with Jerome in Hawaii at the Pro Bowl. On our way to practice each day from our hotel, I shared a car with Jerome, Mike Irvin, and Pat Swilling of New Orleans. I still have a picture of all of us in Hawaii. When I look at it, my heart drops. I can't believe Jerome is gone.

About three weeks later, in the first part of training camp, the Raiders traveled to Austin to practice against us. Tempers were short in the muggy afternoon heat, and the Raiders were trying their best to intimidate us. That's why Jimmy invited them, I think. He knew how physical the Raiders were, how downright nasty at times, and Jimmy wanted to see if we could play the same game. Judging from the number of fights that week, apparently we could.

■　■　■

As that summer kept rolling along, we still had several key veterans holding out. This may have been the start of Jimmy's frustration with Jerry. Jimmy wanted his players in Austin, concentrating on football, not sitting home in a squabble with our owner.

In our first exhibition game, on August 2, we played the Houston Oilers in Tokyo. I enjoyed myself on this trip, but some of our players couldn't wait to get back, and Jimmy had never wanted to go in the first place. When it's time for football, Jimmy's not big on extracurriculars. When he first heard about Japan, he wasn't keen on the sixteen-hour flight, or disrupting our practice routine, or holding numerous press conferences.

Before we left for Japan, Jimmy had made this clear to the newspapers and TV. When some of our players followed Jimmy's lead, Jerry Jones defended the trip in the *Dallas Morning News*. First Jerry said we needed a break from the training camp grind, which I thought made no sense. What's more grinding than flying to Tokyo and back? Later on in his statements, I thought Jerry came much closer to the real point.

Jerry was quoted, "Besides, all expenses are paid, and the Cowboys will receive in excess of three hundred thousand dollars from ESPN for this appearance."

Not wanting to drag his team to a distant part of the world, how was Jimmy *supposed* to feel when he read that? Because on top of the ESPN money, Jerry might have been hoping to make more deals, accumulate more wealth, by showing off *his* Dallas Cowboys to Japanese businessmen. That's Jerry's right as owner of this team. But this is the type of thing I think could have turned off Jimmy. From what I could gather, he always felt football should come before money.

EMMITT SMITH

Normally we play four exhibition games; that, year the Tokyo game gave us a fifth. Though we lost our first three, nobody seemed alarmed. Jimmy's first year in Dallas, his team went 3–1 in exhibitions, then finished 1–15 in the regular season. Jimmy altered his philosophy after that. He'd only point to winning our last two exhibition games. Otherwise Jimmy looked at the bigger picture: How much progress was our team making? Was it enough to start the regular season winning? To fill potential holes, did he need to make any last-minute deals?

Personally, I take my preseason training very seriously, but the games are another matter. I wouldn't even play if the choice were mine. Since I have to, my main goal is staying healthy. In my opinion, the NFL needs only one exhibition game (or at the most, two). In 1992, with our five exhibition games, sixteen more in the regular season, and three in the playoffs, the Dallas Cowboys played twenty-four games. That's a lot of chances for players to get injured, and for NFL fans to miss out when those players do. Since they don't count for anything anyway, why not chop off a few games at the beginning?

On August 27, we made one of those last-minute trades I mentioned. In exchange for a second-round pick in 1993 and a third-round pick the next year, San Francisco traded us Charles Haley. I was stunned when I heard the news. I thought our front office had lost its mind.

I'd heard all the gossip and rumors—Charles was nothing but trouble in San Francisco. Since I have no idea how true those stories were, I won't repeat them. But I had my own personal glimpse of Charles Haley. In 1990, Charles

THE EMMITT ZONE

had 16 sacks, was named NFC Defensive Player of the Year, and ended up his season at the Pro Bowl. I was a rookie that year and also went to Hawaii. The Pro Bowl is normally very mellow, a chance to befriend some guys from other teams. But over the course of that week, Charles Haley talked trash about *everyone*. Some of the Eagles became so enraged, they seemed like they they wanted to jump him.

When I heard Charles was suddenly a Cowboy, my first reaction was: Oh my God. They don't know what they just got themselves into.

When I heard how much he signed for, I thought: How can we pay somebody else's light bill when we can't even pay our own?

At $1.4 million for 1992, Charles was now the highest-paid Cowboy. Meanwhile, Michael Irvin still wasn't signed.

But Charles Haley surprised me. After he and Jimmy sat down for a long private talk, Charles came into our locker room fairly restrained. I don't want to sugarcoat him: When the wrong mood strikes Charles, he can still be a royal pain in the butt. But he's also very funny and highly intelligent. When my mom attends our games, Charles treats her with the utmost respect.

In terms of the trade, I got over my reservations quickly. I still felt it was wrong to sign Charles before Mike, but I also couldn't deny his value to us. Especially in big games, Charles is hell on quarterbacks. That's not all he does, though. At 6-5 and 245 pounds, his power and speed can distress an entire offense.

About one week later, just four days before we would

open against the Redskins, Michael Irvin finally signed. After staying in touch with him throughout training camp, I was extremely happy for him. I was also pleased for myself and for my teammates. Now that we had Mike back, I felt we would go to the Super Bowl that season.

Why shouldn't we go? The season before, while still learning Norv Turner's system, our offense had gone from last in the league to ninth, and our team had advanced to the second round of the playoffs. Now that we knew Norv's system more completely, I expected our offense to lead the league. Defensively, to go with our youth and speed and picking up Charles Haley, we also traded for strong safety Thomas Everett. Once Thomas worked himself into the starting lineup, nobody could remove him. In a rare combination, he became one of our biggest hitters *and* safest tacklers.

■ ■ ■

After Michael came in, our center, Mark Stepnoski, signed later that week. With our entire roster now under contract, my agent and I went back to Jerry Jones. We wanted him to make good on his statement in June: He would take care of me after signing all the others.

Jerry essentially told us: "Okay, we'll get it done." But nothing happened that September. So I told my agent, "Forget it. Don't even try and renegotiate now. The season's already started. I'll just fly with what I have and then we'll see what happens."

In Texas Stadium, in a game being heavily hyped by ABC, we started our run for it all on September 7. In the

THE EMMITT ZONE

first *Monday Night Football* game of the year, the Redskins were coming in as Super Bowl champs. In that week's *Sports Illustrated*, we had just been picked as a bona fide contender.

I couldn't wait to get out there that Monday night. These are the spotlighted games I think I perform my best in.

On the Redskins' first possession, our defense stuffed them deep in their own end. As the Redskins tried to punt, Ike Holt burst through and blocked the ball out of the end zone. Ike's play was big for several reasons: It gave us 2 points on a safety. It swung us the early momentum. And it galvanized our crowd. Our fans turned so loud and vocal—and stayed that way all evening—I couldn't believe I was playing in Texas Stadium.

Normally, I think most of our fans are much too proper. One game, I recall sitting on our bench thinking, Man, this stadium is asleep; we could really use some extra fan support. When I turned toward the stands, the people right behind us were dressed to kill. They were also just sitting and staring—as if they were at a movie. Then I looked above them, up in the cheaper seats. Although I could barely hear them, it *looked* like the fans up there were screaming their lungs out. I thought, Too bad—the fans who get into it most are so far back they can't help us.

The season before, Washington's defense had ranked third in the NFL. In our Monday night opener this year, our offense totaled 390 yards. After missing all of training camp and preseason, Mike Irvin caught 5 passes for 89 yards. Troy threw for 216 yards and 1 touchdown. I fin-

EMMITT SMITH

ished with 140 yards on 27 carries. On defense we allowed only 75 yards rushing, and our pass rushers kept pressure on Mark Rypien all night. In a great way to start our quest, we defeated the Super Bowl champions 23–10.

Then we almost blew it severely the next week in New York. With the Cowboys leading 34–0 early in the third quarter, our offense ground to a halt the rest of the ball game. Phil Simms and his receivers, running their two-minute offense the whole second half, brought the Giants all the way back to 34–28. Our defense regained its balance just in time, as safety James Washington stopped their last drive with an interception. But Jimmy was hot in our locker room afterwards. Jimmy hates mental lapses, and he told us he saw several on both sides of the ball. Nobody disagreed.

Back at Texas Stadium on Sunday, Michael Irvin lit up the Cardinals for 8 receptions, 210 yards, and 3 touchdowns. In the process, I guess he talked all afternoon to their cornerback, Lorenzo Lynch. Not that Michael ever needs a reason to woof, but Lynch apparently brought this on himself. Before the game started, he told James Washington: "Michael Irvin will not catch a pass today." James told Lynch: "Get real. The man's gonna catch eight passes against you." Then James told Mike, of course, and Mike proceeded to own Lorenzo Lynch.

Actually, Lynch knocked down the first pass that came to Mike. Then Lynch made his second verbal mistake of the day: He got up in Michael's face and told him, "See? It's gonna be like this all day."

The very next time Mike got the football, he shook a

tackle by Lynch and went 87 yards for his first TD. When our offense came back on the field, Mike told Lynch, "You're right, hoss. It *is* gonna be like this all day."

Later that game, Mike caught another pass on Lynch, and they wound up tumbling down along our sideline. Fixing a strap on his glove, Mike took his time getting up. But that wasn't the real reason he took his time. Mike knew that Lynch was still sitting right behind him. And without ever looking at him, Mike said over his shoulder: "You might as well stay here on this sideline. Those are grown men out there, so all little boys need to stay on the side. You just can't cover me, son. I'm killing you, boy."

By that point in the game, Lynch wasn't saying anything anymore. Mike had used him so badly, I was almost feeling sorry for the guy.

With our three straight wins in the NFC East—the best division in football the past several years—some people were now calling us the team to beat. But those people didn't live in Philadelphia, where the Eagles were also 3–0, and where the fans were lying in wait for the hated Cowboys. In fact, on the same day that Michael Irvin had schooled Lorenzo Lynch, the Eagles' fans had been screaming, "We want Dallas!" They were playing the Denver Broncos at the time.

Since both teams had a bye on September 27, the people in Philly had two weeks to whip themselves into a frenzy. All over the newspapers and TV, they were treating this game like the Eagles' Super Bowl. Jimmy Johnson, at the same time, was keeping things in perspective. Jimmy intended to win, but he didn't want our whole season rest-ing on this. It was only our fourth game, the Eagles were always hard for us to beat, and they were playing that year with great emotion. Stunned by the death of their friend and teammate Jerome Brown, the Eagles had dedicated their season to him.

Though I understood Jimmy's tactics, I had no trepidation at all before this game. I truly believed we'd whip them, and I think most of my teammates had the same mind-set. If anything, we went into Veterans Stadium overconfident.

I'll never forget walking out of the tunnel that night. With the lights already turned on, all I could see in the stands was a blur of pulsating green. On our first play from scrimmage, Reggie White caught Troy Aikman unprotected. Troy tried avoiding the sack and the refs called intentional grounding. The Vet always rocks when the Cowboys are there, and now the fans went ballistic. After I went nowhere on second and 22, Troy got intercepted by John Booty, who ran the football back to our 14-yard line. Randall Cunningham scored two plays later, and just that fast the Eagles led 7–0.

When our offense came back out and showed some character, driving 84 yards for a game-tying TD, we did something I thought was impossible: We subdued Veterans Stadium. Nobody scored at all in the second quarter, and we went into halftime trailing only 10–7. I thought things were looking good. Thanks mostly to our defense, all the Eagles had to show was a 3-point lead.

I was wrong. In the second half our offense self-destructed. Twice we turned the ball over to give them good field position, and twice the Eagles responded by scoring touchdowns.

Both of those touchdowns were scored by Herschel Walker. In the past two weeks of Cowboy-Eagle hype, much had been made of Herschel playing against his old team. Only Hershel knows if he saw this game as payback. But in any case he played well, with 86 yards and those 2 key second-half touchdowns. Herschel's performance didn't surprise me at all. I've always considered him a quality runner. Although he isn't shifty, he's powerful and fast and he always moves north and south.

Keith Byars scored again with three minutes left, and Philadephia beat us 31–7. Although embarrassed and disappointed, we all agreed with Jimmy after the game: There was no reason to let this crush us. The Eagles outplayed us that night. But they'd also cashed in on several of our mistakes, and we'd actually outgained them in total yardage. In another big NFC East game, we'd see the Eagles again in only five weeks. This time they'd have to come to Dallas.

■ ■ ■

Jimmy Johnson was right: The Eagles spent so much energy on their "October Super Bowl," they lost three of their next four games. Our team went on to win five in a row.

The first of those wins came at home against Seattle. We romped 27–0, although I averaged only 3.5 yards per carry. The primary reason for that was Cortez Kennedy. Making tackles from sideline to sideline, he was far and away their best player that game. At one point in our huddle, I said, "Who in the *hell* is Cortez Kennedy? This guy is all over the place."

After we beat Kansas City, our record was 5–1. On the downside, I hadn't gained 100 yards in four of our first six games. Still, I didn't get rattled. I said to myself: "Be patient. Your big game is coming soon. Just be ready when the opportunity comes."

It happened on October 25 against the Raiders, our close personal friends from our training camp in July. In the first game I ever played at the Coliseum, I had 3 touchdowns and 152 yards. I also fell in love with the Coliseum grass, which was nice and short and not at all slick. As you've probably gathered by now, I prefer grass to artificial turf. Turf doesn't give and grass does, so it's easier on the legs. I also think my cuts are sharper on grass.

With 91,505 fans packed into the Coliseum, this was the largest crowd of my career, and the largest crowd ever to watch the Dallas Cowboys. The odd thing was, about 40,000 of those fans appeared to be rooting for us. Toward the end of the game, I could've sworn I saw more blue than silver and black. I knew the Dallas Cowboys had fans in every city, but that kind of blew me away.

Even though we never let the Raiders find out, I went into that game with a painful lower back. Three weeks earlier, in Philadelphia, I had taken a helmet in the back from Andre Waters. He came in late with what I considered a cheap shot. I've never quite understood this, because Andre can really play. If he would just cut all that foolishness out, stop trying to damage people, he could lose that reputation of his.

In our 28–13 win, one of the Raiders delivered what I would call a cheap shot of his own. On my second touchdown run, a draw play up the middle, linebacker Ricky Ellis came flying over the top with his arm extended, clotheslined my head, and almost knocked me cold. I'm not sure how, but I managed to stay on my feet and find the end zone. Things worked out much better in my final score of the day. With just more than three minutes left, I broke one for 26 yards and barely got touched. I don't know which Raider he nailed, but Daryl Johnston laid somebody out on this play.

I also recall one collision with Ronnie Lott, the Hall of Fame–bound strong safety. After Ronnie rushed up and hit me, I spun and bounced off and ran for a few more yards. The next time I played against him, Ronnie Lott was a New York Jet. I kiddingly told him before our game, "Now, you take it easy on me." Ronnie said, "Shoot! I hit you a year ago with everything I had, and you just ran right through it." Coming from him, it meant a lot.

On November 1 at Texas Stadium, in our second crack at the Philadelphia Eagles, I lost a fumble in the first quarter. In the course of that season, including the playoffs, I would carry the ball 444 times; I would fumble only five times, losing two. Maybe because I fumble the ball so rarely, each of them sticks in my mind. This time, Clyde Simmons swiped at the football from behind. I never even saw him.

That didn't make me feel any less miserable. I should have been holding the ball with a firmer grip. I knew how big the Eagles were on the swipe move.

EMMITT SMITH

That's why, on the first play after my fumble, I felt so relieved when Larry Brown intercepted Randall Cunningham. Let me repeat that: Larry Brown intercepted Randall Cunningham. You see, Larry doesn't make a lot of interceptions.

But Larry caught this one and saved my behind.

With both offenses stalling and us leading 3–0 at halftime, the Eagles seemed to be more concerned than we were. To start the third quarter, their coach, Rich Kotite, yanked Randall Cunningham in favor of Jim McMahon. I had mixed emotions about that. Without Randall in there, the Eagles lost a significant part of their offense, and their charisma. But the season before this one, our team had lost several times against backup quarterbacks. When McMahon took them right down the field for an 80-yard touchdown drive, the Eagles led 7–3, and I thought, Oh Lord, here we go again.

Remember what I said about staying patient, back when I didn't reach 100 yards in four of our first six games? In the first half against the Eagles, I gained 48 yards. Not a terrible half, but nothing explosive. After halftime, keeping my cool, I had another 115, for a total of 163.

Fifty-one of those came on a gift from the Eagles. We were deep in our own territory in the third quarter, when Norv Turner called an inside handoff to me. All we wanted was a little more breathing room, but their inside linebacker blitzed and ran right past me. Suddenly I saw a massive hole straight up the middle.

Once I got into the secondary, I quickly cut to the right to avoid the free safety. I turned upfield and got hit by their right cornerback, but bounced off him and just kept running. Fifty-one yards downfield, I was knocked out-of-bounds by Wes Hopkins and Eric Allen. I made a nice run, but I also got lucky. Gaffes like that don't happen often when you're playing Philadelphia.

Neither do long physical drives that mostly stay on the ground. But that's just what our offense pulled off in the fourth quarter. With a 13–10 lead and the ball at our own 20, we went 80 yards in eight plays to ice the ball game. I had 45 yards, but the real heroes were our offensive linemen. Luck had nothing to do with it this time. Our offensive linemen just beat up the Eagles.

Though all our linemen excelled that Sunday in Dallas, our right tackle, Erik Williams, had to block Reggie White. In their first meeting, back in Philly, Reggie had sacked Troy Aikman twice. This time Erik held Reggie to no sacks, 2 tackles, and 1 assist. Erik was elated after the game. At age twenty-four, in his second year in the league, he wanted to prove himself and go to the Pro Bowl, and holding down Reggie White was a major step. To make it even sweeter, Erik grew up two miles from Veterans Stadium. As a child he wanted to be like Reggie White.

Our win against the Eagles made us 7–1. This gave us a two-game lead in the NFC East, and our confidence level was soaring. On Sunday afternoon, November 8, we crushed the Lions 37–3. On Saturday morning, November 7, Michael Irvin had missed our flight from Dallas to Detroit.

Players missing team planes almost never happens with us. Unless, that is, we pull a gag on a rookie. In 1991,

Curvin Richards missed a flight to our opening game in Cleveland, because everyone said we were flying from Love Field in Dallas. While Curvin was over at Love, the rest of us were leaving from Dallas–Forth Worth.

Now, around 10:30 A.M. before our flight on Saturday, I had no idea why Michael's seat was empty. I was sitting next to our tight end, Alfredo Roberts, one of Mike's best friends, and Alfredo also didn't know what happened to him. *Nobody* seemed to know where Michael was, including Jimmy Johnson. After we sat on the runway a couple minutes, Jimmy ordered our pilot to leave without him.

When Mike arrived that night by commercial flight, I don't recall what his explanation was. I do remember that all the players razzed him, but nobody seemed upset. Mike has always been a team player through and through; one missed flight didn't change that.

It's Jimmy who made the rules, though, and one of the big things he stressed was being on time. On Sunday against the Lions, Jimmy kept Mike on the bench for our opening series. He also fined him for missing our flight, but then Jimmy seemed to forget it all pretty quickly. For one thing, Mike caught 5 passes against the Lions for 114 yards. For another, I don't think Jimmy was capable of staying mad at Mike. Not after all they'd been through in Dallas and Miami.

Going into our home game against the Rams, our ball club seemed to be peaking. Since losing to the Eagles the first week of October, we'd won five in a row to put us at 8–1. In our last game we blew out Detroit, a team that had pounded on us twice in a row. So how could the 3–6 Rams beat us 27–23? It was mostly Jim Everett and penalties.

Preparing for this game, none of us dreamed the Rams would score 27 points. In our last *five* games, our defense had allowed only 36 points combined. Also, Norv Turner had coached for the Rams before coming to Dallas. Not only did he know their offense, he'd incorporated a lot of it into ours. We figured that gave us an edge against the Rams. All season long, at practice, our defense looked at an offense that mirrored the Rams'. When Sunday came, we didn't see how their offense could surprise us.

Jim Everett sabotaged our plans. He was so hot that game, so clutch, they didn't need to surprise us. Even when we caught him off guard with a blitz, Everett threw the ball just before we could sack him. As our defensive coordinator, Dave Wannstedt, said, "Jim Everett put on a clinic."

We might have won anyway, if we didn't stymie ourselves with so many important penalties. In a game decided by only 4 points, Jimmy figured our 60 yards in penalties gave the Rams 13 points and cost us 4. As you can imagine, Jimmy wasn't real pleased doing the math.

Our record was still 8–2, but it wasn't as safe as it sounded. We had the Cardinals at Sun Devil Stadium on Sunday, the Giants at home on Thanksgiving four days later, then road games at Denver, Washington, and Atlanta. All during practice the week before the Cardinals, it was obvious that our coaching staff was stressed. My teammates and I weren't as concerned, though. Football coaches are paid to get paranoid, players are paid to perform.

Our players all realized we blew it against the Rams. But we also knew how good our football team was.

■ ■ ■

Maybe we were wrong and the coaches were right. We beat the Cardinals 16–10 in Tempe, but our offense looked horrendous, and nine of our points came on Lin Elliott field goals. My entire career, I'd never seen a front four so doggone big. No kidding around, both their tackles and both their ends must have gone over 300 pounds. Phoenix also came out in a defense we hadn't prepared for, and all in all it got ugly out in the desert. For the first time since I became a Cowboy, I was struggling just to get past the line of scrimmage. On 23 carries I gained only 84 yards, and Jimmy blasted our linemen after the game. "As long as I'm coach of the Dallas Cowboys," he yelled, "we will NOT average less than three yards a carry again!"

With the Giants coming on Thursday, reporters wanted to know what was wrong with our offense. Norv Turner told them, "We're just in a lull. People are taking away some things we've had success with. They're doubling Michael and committing to stop Emmitt. It's going to be tough from here on out."

It certainly would, and we needed to lift our game to another level. In the NFL, playing just well enough to win is a recipe for disaster.

At first, with the Cowboys leading the Giants 9–3 at halftime, our game on Thanksgiving looked like a real

THE EMMITT ZONE

yawner. You think you get bored watching football games like this? Well, so do the players. This particular game was embarrassing, too. On national TV, Thanksgiving and all, we wanted to put on a much better show.

At least New York had an excuse for their sluggish offense: Both Phil Simms and Jeff Hostetler were out with injuries. By the way, remember that "quarterback controversy" up there, with some folks pushing Simms and some pushing Hostetler? Man, both those guys are winners. Rather than comparing them all the time, the people in New York should have counted their blessings.

Anyway, I found myself getting hot in the third quarter. With the score still 9–3 Cowboys, Troy threw a little swing pass my way. First I put a fake on their cornerback, Reyna Thompson. Then I cut to the sideline, headed straight for the goal, cut back to the middle, and wound up getting knocked into the end zone. My 26-yard TD put us ahead 16–3.

On our next possession, I broke what we call a Slant G for 68 yards and another TD. Designed almost like a trap play, it worked exactly the way we had practiced it all week: Nate Newton pulled right and kicked out the defensive end. Erik Williams blocked down on the inside linebacker. Daryl Johnston smashed into the gap between them. After taking one short step toward the sideline—to make it look like a sweep—I slanted straight for the hole. Just as our offensive line coach, Tony Wise, had predicted, I went through so fast the Giants barely saw me. It was beautiful: The coaches called the right play against the right defense. The blockers all did their jobs. I went 68 yards without being touched.

EMMITT SMITH

For the finishing touch that Thanksgiving day, Troy hit Alvin Harper to make it 30–3. Against a good Giant defense, we had just scored 21 points in twenty-four minutes. It looked to me like our offense was back on track.

■ ■ ■

Twelve weeks into the NFL season—and coming off games on Sunday and then on Thursday—my body was getting that numb sensation again. As a running back who carries the ball a lot, I find it always happens to me this time of year, and it's always strange. I feel the hits, but I don't. My body's already so battered, it's like they're beating a piece of meat.

Fortunately, we had ten days off until our next game, against Denver. It was about this time that Jerry Jones called me into his Valley Ranch office. He said he was ready to renegotiate now.

Jerry handed me a memo. Then the conversation went something like this:

"This is the same exact contract that Barry Sanders has."

"What are you trying to tell me? I'm the exact same player that Barry Sanders is?"

"No, we feel you're better than Barry Sanders."

"Wait a minute, Jerry. If you think I'm better than Barry, why don't you pay me that way? I led the league in rushing last year. I have a good chance to lead the league again. I was the first Cowboy of this era to go to the Pro Bowl. I went back again last year, and I think I'll be there this year. I don't want what Barry Sanders is getting paid. I want more than that. I want to be the highest-paid running back. I want my salary to reflect my performance."

When I plead my case, I plead my case. I don't hold back, but I also stick to the point.

Jerry, however, likes talking in circles. And that day he fed me his usual line. I don't know what else to call it.

It was probably the same explanation he gave our assistant coaches, who I'm pretty sure were among the lowest-paid in the league. Several of them are gone now, of course, most notably Dave Wannstedt and Norv Turner. It might have been simply an urge to become head coaches. But working for Jerry Jones, they might also have felt underpaid and underappreciated. One thing I know for certain: When the Cowboys lost Wannstedt and Turner, they lost a lot. But everyone knows that things are done differently here.

That day in Jerry's office, I told him I'd talk to my agent and then get back. I showed Richard Howell the numbers. He agreed they weren't sufficient. After making a counteroffer and getting rejected, I told Richard, "That's it. I don't even want to talk about it again. We've got the meat of our season coming up."

■ ■ ■

As in any other profession, life in the NFL has its ups and downs. One great part is the friends you make on your team. That's why road trips, for me, have never been a drag. On the contrary, I love traveling with our team. Since I have no fear of flying, I even enjoy our plane flights. I'm hanging around my buddies. We're playing cards and dominoes, needling each other and cracking each other up.

EMMITT SMITH

Then we land in another city and get to play pro football. It's not exactly the worst way to make a living. So even though I may harp about things like contracts and value, in other ways I know I've been very lucky.

On December 6, in a snowstorm, our airplane bumped and dipped its way into Denver. At Mile High that season the Broncos were 6–0, but that didn't intimidate us. My teammates and I pride ourselves on being an excellent road team. There's always something satisfying, too, about kicking a team's behind in their own backyard.

Actually, I think our team has sharper focus when we play on the road. The spotlight on the Cowboys burns so intensely in Dallas, at times it can be distracting. The scrutiny doesn't vanish outside of Dallas, but it's nowhere near as relentless. In other cities we're basically just the bad guys.

In this, my first trip to Denver, one thing I did find intimidating was the air. I'd heard about it, but I thought that's all it was—a lotta talk. Then, at our hotel the night before the game, I jogged several flights of stairs to our meeting downstairs. By the bottom floor I was huffing and puffing so bad, I thought: Oh my God! I hope it's not like this tomorrow!

On Sunday afternoon at Mile High, it was also twenty degrees as we took the football field. Having grown up in Florida, I've never liked playing in cold. When it's cold and the air is thin and your lungs feel tight, it doesn't help you much in trying to run the football. Denver's two safeties, Steve Atwater and Dennis Smith, don't help a lot either. Those are some hard-hitting jokers.

Still, we had two advantages that game. Denver had no

THE EMMITT ZONE

more snow after its first storm. And John Elway, the greatest comeback quarterback I've ever seen, was on the sideline with an injured shoulder.

Tommy Maddox, Elway's replacement, threw two early interceptions, which we quickly turned into a 14–0 lead. But Maddox hung tough, particularly for a rookie, and his two touchdown passes kept Denver right in the game. Our own offense, meanwhile, could not run the football. Atwater and Smith, their two big safeties, were coming up on the run like linebackers do. At halftime our lead was only 17–13, and 14 of our points had come after interceptions.

With nine minutes left in the game, we got the football back at our own 23. Denver led 27–24. It was money time.

Troy threw to Daryl Johnston for 6 yards, then I got stopped for no gain. On a key third down and 4, Troy hit Jay Novacek for 11 yards. Then Jay made receptions of 22 and 17. If I recall correctly, the Broncos had Karl Mecklenberg covering Jay. Mecklenberg's a warrior, but he doesn't have the quickness to keep up with Jay. No matter who's covering him, Jay *always* finds a way to get himself open. With that unorthodox running style of his, he lulls people to sleep, then beats them badly. We call Jay "Paycheck," because he's so clutch.

On another huge third down at the Denver 25, Troy hit Michael Irvin for 14 yards to keep us alive. Three plays later, it all came down to third and 2 at the Denver 3. In our huddle I pulled my gloves a little tighter, hoping Norv Turner had called my number. I got what I wanted—the football—but the call itself surprised me. Norv wanted a draw play, unusual when a team is so close to the goal line.

Denver blitzed, I found a hole, and I scored the winning touchdown without getting tackled. We'd gone 77 yards in eleven plays, to come from behind at Mile High, one of the hardest places to win in the NFL. Norv Turner said after the game: "That drive was what Super Bowl seasons are made of."

■　■　■

Thirteen weeks after beating the Redskins on the season's first Monday night game, we played them at RFK on December 13. At 11–2, with three straight wins, we needed a victory there to clinch the NFC East title.

With four minutes left in the game, we led 17–13. The Redskins had fourth and goal at our 2, but a field goal would still leave them down by a point. Mark Rypien threw incomplete and we took over on downs, but our position was still extremely precarious. Backed up to our own goal line, we had to protect the ball and kill some clock.

On first and 10 from our 2, Daryl Johnston ran for 3 yards. On second and 7, Norv Turner daringly called for a pass. As Troy dropped back to throw from inside our end zone, I saw his arm moving forward—just as he got hit by tackle Jason Buck. The ball squirted free and I picked it up. I did it purely by instinct, not because I thought I had to. Since Troy's arm was moving forward, I figured the refs would call this an incomplete pass.

This was all happening fast, remember. And as I grabbed the ball, I got tackled by one of the Redskins in our end zone. At the same moment, I tried handing the ball forward to tight end Alfredo Roberts. I wanted to get

THE EMMITT ZONE

the ball out of our end zone, just in case all this nonsense *wasn't* an incomplete pass.

My plan failed. Miserably. Still in the end zone, the ball hit Alfredo's leg and popped loose again. The Redskins' Danny Copeland recovered for a touchdown. Washington won on that crazy play, 20–17. Looking back on it now, I should have jumped on the football and taken the safety. Even with their two points, the Redskins would still have been losing 17–16.

However, there's no denying the fact that the refs blew this call. In fact, according to what the NFL said later, the refs were wrong twice that play. After watching the film, the league said Troy's arm was moving forward, so the play was an incomplete pass and not a fumble. And when I tried handing the football to Alfredo, the NFL said, my knee was already down. But none of that helped on Sunday at RFK, where the scoreboard still read 20–17, Washington. Down on the field, the refs were telling our players, "Get back, get back," while I was standing there hollering, "Incomplete pass!"

People sometimes ask me: "How far can you go with the refs in terms of language?" Well, I've seen some refs get cussed out and still not throw a flag. As for myself, I swear to you I have never cursed a ref. But I have run a couple over. I did this inadvertently, of course.

On our plane flight back to Dallas, Jimmy came back to our part of the cabin seething. We were so teed off about losing, we weren't even being loud or anything, but Jimmy just went off on the first guy he saw—our backup center, Frank Cornish. Jimmy told Frank to sit his ass in his seat. Tommie Agee and Robert Jones got chewed out next. Jimmy wasn't through. Assistant coaches, flight attendants—Jimmy yelled at them all. Some of our players couldn't believe it was happening. A few got upset and avoided him for a while. How did I feel about it? I considered Jimmy's actions uncalled for. We blew it against the Redskins at RFK; Jimmy blew it on our plane flight.

■　■　■

According to some of the writers who flew on our plane, Jimmy's tirade had damaged our morale. I disagreed. If anything, it reminded us that we couldn't become complacent. With two games left in the regular season, the NFC East title was still at stake.

Though we drilled the Falcons on Sunday, 41–17, we actually started out sloppy. The first carry I had, I popped it for maybe 12 yards. But the refs called it back for holding. Troy completed a pass; the refs called it back for jumping offside. I ran again for positive yardage—illegal procedure on us. If we'd backed up any farther, we might as well have ordered hot dogs—we'd have been sitting up in the stands behind the end zone.

So that's when I did something uncharacteristic: I exploded on my teammates.

"Hey!" I shouted at them in our huddle. "We need this game! You guys planning on getting your heads into it? We lost last week to the Redskins! Let's go ahead and clinch today! Let's get our butts in gear—come on!"

Everyone seemed surprised. One guy, Mark Stepnoski,

looked as if he was angry. Step said, "Just calm down, man! We're gonna be all right! It's early!"

But I was still steaming. I told him, "Shoot, we just got our butts whipped by the 'Skins! Let's get intense!"

Then Troy Aikman took over. In the first half alone, he hit 15 of 17 passes for 196 yards and 2 touchdowns. On most of those plays, I swung out as Troy's third receiver. On some plays I pass-blocked for him. That's always a challenging task from the tailback position. By NFL standards, you're probably not that big. Yet you're often blocking linebackers who are blitzing, people like Lawrence Taylor, Cornelius Bennett, and Wilber Marshall. These people are out to rearrange your quarterback, and if you're in the way they'll punish you too. One time, against the New York Jets, I tried taking on Mo Lords. I stood straight up, and Mo ran right through me. When I staggered back to my feet, I told myself, "Forget it. I'm not staying up on these guys. I'm cutting them at the thigh."

Even though I'm not asked to do it often, I take my pass-blocking seriously. If I can protect our quarterback, I know I've done my duty. If I miss my block and Troy gets stomped, I feel the same way I do when I fumble the ball. Like a sorry dog.

If it was the Troy-and-Mike show in the first half—Mike wound up with 6 catches for 89 yards—I moved onto center stage when those guys were through. I gained 132 yards in the second half, for a total of 174 (at that point my second-best day in the NFL). I also had 2 nifty touchdowns, and on one of those plays I outran Deion Sanders. Okay, so I didn't outrun him. But he didn't catch me either.

EMMITT SMITH

This wasn't the first game I played against Deion Sanders. My freshman year at Florida, he and his Florida State teammates visited us at Gainesville. On our first series back then, I took a toss right and screeched up the sideline for 55 yards or so. Deion caught me and ran me out-of-bounds. I knew the guy was fast, but I didn't know he was a blur. Deion made several exciting defensive plays that day. He was an All-American and then some.

Today I know Deion personally, and face-to-face, away from the football field and the TV cameras, he isn't Prime Time. He's a gentle, humble person. As for Deion playing two sports, why does that bother some people so much? Whose life is it anyway—theirs or Deion's? I felt the same way when Michael Jordan began playing baseball. Some people actually seemed insulted by that. I thought that was ridiculous. Lighten up! Let the man work in whatever field he wants. That's what this country is based on.

Hypothetically speaking, I'll take it one step further. If I could play baseball as well as I play football, I might do the same thing Michael Jordan is doing. I've been playing football since I was a little boy. I've played for two Super Bowl teams. I've proven what I can do as an individual. And I've played for Jimmy Johnson, maybe the best football coach on this planet. Why not test myself someday in another arena?

Besides, baseball players tend to have longer careers. They don't suffer the kind of arthritis that football players do. Their pension plan and benefit package is stronger, and their union is light-years ahead of the National Football League Players Association. I know our union is

THE EMMITT ZONE

trying, and I support them. But at this stage the NFL owners still dominate them. In baseball, the union has genuine
clout.

■　■　■

Before we played the Bears to close the regular season, I
was named to the Pro Bowl my third year in a row. For the
second straight year I was voted in as a starter. Jay Novacek also made it in as a starter, and Mike Irvin, Troy Aikman, Nate Newton, and Mark Stepnoski were all reserves.

That was all terrific—for our offense. On our defensive
unit, not one of our players made it. Our guys were teed off
and I didn't blame them. When the final stats came out,
our defense was ranked first in the NFL. How can the best
defense in the league not feature a single player in the Pro
Bowl? The good news was, our guys didn't mope around.
They took their anger and slapped it on our opponents. In
the four games after the Pro Bowl announcements were
made, our defense allowed an average of 15.2 points a
game. This included three postseason games. Meaning our
defense was doing a job on the NFL's premier teams.

■　■　■

For a game that had no bearing on the playoffs, what *didn't*
happen that Sunday against Chicago?

1. After a long and brilliant and dignified career, Mike Singletary played his final game.
2. We were killing the Bears and then started
   playing poorly.

EMMITT SMITH

3. Jimmy Johnson got mad at us about that, and he also got upset with Jerry Jones, when Jerry went strolling with friends on our sideline at Texas Stadium.
4. With 131 yards—and 1,713 for the season—I won my second consecutive rushing title.

On the NFL's final Sunday, I needed to come from behind to beat Pittsburgh's Barry Foster, a strong, determined runner whom I admire. Barry had played at noon and we didn't start until three, so I knew I needed 109 yards to beat him. One of the people in my path, literally, was Chicago's Mike Singletary. What a middle linebacker that guy was. If he doesn't make the Hall of Fame . . . ah, forget it. Mike is a lock.

I'll never forget the first time I played against him, at Chicago the season before in the NFC playoffs. On our first offensive play, I was standing at the back of our I formation. I looked across the line and saw these two big eyes popping out of Mike's helmet. It was cold in Chicago that day. Steam came out of his mouth and his cheeks were puffed out and red. Singletary was rocking right and left, rocking left and right, and I looked at him and silently said to myself: "This joker's crazy. He's done lost his mind."

It was a trip! If Mike didn't capture the essence of pro football, then nobody has or ever will. He's one guy I'd really have loved to play with.

This year against the Bears, in the third quarter, I ran 31 yards for a touchdown to give me the rushing title. I was so elated to win it back-to-back, I kept on running all the way into our tunnel. I wasn't about to lose that football, either. As I always do whenever I score a touchdown, I put this one in a trunk we keep near our bench. On Monday, our equipment managers would give it back to me. But first they'd mark it up with all the vital statistics. December 27, 1993. Thirty-one yards against the Chicago Bears. That type of stuff.

At that point Jimmy pulled me out the game, so I took off my shoulder pads, sat on our bench, and said thanks to our offensive linemen: Mark Tuinei, Nate Newton, Mark Stepnoski, John Gesek, Erik Williams, Frank Cornish, and Kevin Gogan. When I won my first rushing title the year before, I gave all our starting linemen Rolex watches. This time I gave them paintings. They already knew the rushing title was partly theirs. This was just my way of saying I knew it too.

As the third quarter ended, our lead had stretched to 27–0. That's when Jerry brought Prince Bandar down on our sideline. There were several others in their group too, but the only ones I recognized were Jerry and the prince. Parading around our sideline, introducing some of our players to his entourage, Jerry seemed to be basking in front of our crowd.

Jerry does this frequently at our home games. Strange as it sounds, he treats our football team like some kind of show. And Jerry Jones is the star—at least in his own eyes.

How do the players respond when Jerry and his friends take their Sunday afternoon stroll along our sideline?

Some players roll their eyes. Some are too busy to care. Some ask out loud to nobody in particular: "What are these people doing down here with us? Why's Jerry even down here?"

In the fourth quarter that game, the sloppiness started. First my backup, Curvin Richards, fumbled. That didn't hurt us, since we got the ball right back on an interception. But then Steve Beuerlein, relieving Troy, was also intercepted. After the Bears scored their first TD, Curvin Richards fumbled again on our next series. This fumble was scooped up by Chris Zorich, who ran the ball 42 yards for another quick Bear touchdown.

I felt horrible watching that second fumble by Curvin, because I knew just how irate Jimmy would get. And when Jimmy cut Curvin the following day, even though we were about to go into the playoffs, I wasn't all that surprised. Curvin had other fumbles that season, and Jimmy doesn't keep runners who turn the ball over. But I still felt lousy for Curvin. This league can be really cold.

Jimmy scolded us after the Bears game for getting so careless. Then, after he addressed the press, he reportedly went straight to Jerry's private suite. Only Jimmy and Jerry can tell you what was said there, but it probably had something to do with Jerry's flashy entrance while Jimmy was still coaching football.

At least that's what the Dallas media later said. As for the players during this time, that was really as close as we got to their so-called feud. It may sound like a cop-out, but we honestly didn't know if they were fighting back then. Basically, we were just like everyone else: We heard stories about them clashing, but were never sure what to make of them. There's always so much gossip in this league, most players learn to tune the majority out.

Later, things would change: The rift between Jimmy and Jerry would start to show.

12
SUPER THE
FIRST TIME

On December 27 we beat the Bears. Two days earlier, I had spent Christmas Day in Dallas going to meetings and practice. Being away from home on Christmas is a fact of NFL life. I've accepted that now, but my rookie year it was tough. Used to spending the holiday with my family, I found myself getting homesick and sentimental.

Christmas was always nice when I was a kid. The seven of us would start off the holiday at our house, just my mother and father and brothers and sisters and I. Then we'd go to my grandparents' house and meet up with even more relatives. Then we'd celebrate again at our other grandparents' house. We didn't go crazy with presents since we didn't have that much money, but there was always a lot of delicious food. Most years, a number of my cousins would come in from out of town. They were all getting big, like me, and we'd eat at every stop until we couldn't breathe.

■ ■ ■

After the Bears game I figured: What the heck? With a bye week in the opening round of the playoffs, Jimmy had given us all a couple days off, so I hopped on a plane and landed in Pensacola. I stayed in my old bedroom, spent some quiet time with my family, and tried not to dwell too much on professional football. I'd be back in the thick of it soon enough.

On January 3, the Eagles won in the wild-card round, so they would play us in Dallas the following Sunday. As usual, the Eagles came in talking. Their tight end, Keith Byars, simply predicted a win. Speaking of our first game that year, their 31–7 victory at the Vet, their linebacker, Byron Evans, said, "Nobody put it to 'em like we did, and they know it." Then their safety, Andre Waters, said of me in particular: "Two of us are going to walk on the field, but only one of us is going to walk off. They're going to have to carry him off."

That was a little nasty even for Andre, but I had a feeling something like this was coming. Earlier that season Andre had broken his leg. I was quoted at the time: "What goes around comes around. When you do ugly things to others, when you try and hurt other players, it's bound to come back at you." The quote was perfectly accurate; I won't deny that. But from what I was told by people I trust, one Dallas reporter then distorted my words. Going straight to Andre Waters for a reaction, he told him I said I was "glad" he'd broken his leg.

Even knowing what possibly provoked it, Andre's statement annoyed me. This game is inherently violent. All of us understand this and accept it. But most players have no interest in doing serious damage; they know how much work it takes just to get to the NFL. So whether it's Andre or anyone else, I hate it when players talk about taking someone out. There's just no call for that. At any level of football.

Did I use Andre's comments to fuel my motivation?

Nope. This was Dallas-Philadelphia in the playoffs. When that's not enough to fire me up, that's the day I'll retire.

On January 10, 1993, in the first playoff game in Dallas in almost ten years, we dominated the Eagles, 34–10. After letting up a field goal on their first possession, our defense shut them out until the game's final minute, when Randall Cunningham threw an 18-yard TD pass. Before that, our defense sacked him five times. Randall told reporters after the game: "Every time I saw somebody open for even a second, the Cowboys were back in my face."

Offensively, Troy threw two touchdown passes in the first half. Out of my 114 yards rushing, I had 69 in the third quarter alone. Our first series that quarter, I broke a draw play for 23 yards and my first postseason touchdown. This gave me 19 TDs for the season, put us in front of the Eagles 24–3, and also put a hush on most of their talking. Up until

THE EMMITT ZONE

then Andre Waters was saying to me, "I'm gonna getcha, I'm gonna getcha." I'd been telling Andre, "Just shut your mouth and play football."

According to *Sports Illustrated* that week, our 34–10 win was "the worst playoff drubbing in Philly history, and only one thing was left to do in the wake of it: ask Waters if he still meant all those nasty things he'd said about Smith.

"What can I say?" Andre replied. "Today he showed he's a great running back."

Then the writer topped it off with: "So what were Smith's back-to-back rushing titles? Chopped liver?"

And from that playoff game on, the feud between Andre and me has quieted down. I even tried helping him up once, when he almost knocked himself out trying to hit me. Andre went flying into his own player instead, crashed to the ground, and didn't look too healthy. When I reached out my hand to give him a lift, Andre refused my help.

What can I tell you? I said our feud was calming down. I didn't say it was over.

■　■　■

Next stop Candlestick Park, for the NFC Championship Game. With 14 wins in the regular season, compared to our 13, San Francisco had secured the home field advantage.

Back in Dallas the week before the game, I couldn't turn on my TV without seeing "the catch." Ten years earlier, in the 1982 NFC title game in San Francisco, Joe Montana had hit Dwight Clark in the right corner of the end zone to beat the Dallas Cowboys, 28–27. Some people called "the catch" a turning point for both teams. In the seasons to come, the Cowboys got old and consistently missed the playoffs, tumbling all the way down to 1–15. Winning four Super Bowls in four tries, San Francisco went on to be dubbed the "team of the eighties."

The catch, the catch, the catch. Who cared about the catch? I was twelve years old at the time; I don't think I even watched the game.

So we came up with our own theme that week: Forget the catch. Forget the past. We're the 1992 Dallas Cowboys. We're the top team in pro football right here and now.

That's not to say we took San Francisco lightly. Most of us considered them the second-best team in the league. So if we could knock them off Sunday, we thought we could also handle Miami or Buffalo, the only two teams left in the AFC. In short, we thought we'd win it all if we beat San Francisco.

On offense, the 49ers were stacked. At quarterback they had Steve Young, the NFL MVP. Young was backed up by Joe Montana and Steve Bono, meaning their third-string QB was better than many teams' starters. But of those three quarterbacks, I considered Steve Young our biggest concern. In today's NFL, with how fast and quick the pass rushers are, mobility in the pocket is essential, and no quarterback can move the way Steve Young does. He can hurt a defense two ways: by scrambling around while his receivers get open, and by running the ball himself when he isn't contained.

His primary target was Jerry Rice, who I think is one of the two best receivers in football. The other is Michael

Irvin. Michael would like me to say he stands alone. But with Jerry's great hands and speed, his ability to break tackles, I just can't bring myself to call either man the best. In fact, sometimes I'll tease Mike about Jerry Rice. If Mike drops a pass I look over and tell him, "Hey! Jerry Rice woulda caught that!" Then, if I should get caught in a hole just as it closes, Michael will say, "What happened there, hoss? Barry Sanders would've gotten through that one."

John Taylor played at the other wide receiver, and John is an unsung hero over there. So is their fullback, Tom Rathman, who will not only block you into next week, but can run and catch passes too. Their tailback was Ricky Watters, big and tough and very enthusiastic. Unlike some college stars who fizzle out in the pros, Ricky's even better now than he was at Notre Dame.

Defensively that year, San Francisco played the run well but seemed vulnerable to the pass. So I knew going in that our offense would come out passing. I had no problem with that. With as good as their offense was, I felt our biggest key was keeping them off the field. If that meant more passing than running, then so be it. I also knew my own time would come later on, once our passing game had softened them up for the run. And this, in my view, is what makes the Dallas Cowboys so potent on offense. If you gang up on the run, Novacek, Harper, and Irvin will hurt you with the pass. If you double up on our receivers, Moose and I will make you pay on the ground. As Jimmy Johnson used to put it: "A team has to make up its mind against the Cowboys. Do they want to die slowly by the run, or die by lethal injection when we pass?" Jimmy had it right. In my opinion, no offense in the league can match us for balance.

Did I say balance? The Friday night we arrived in San Francisco, I actually felt the earth move.

I *saw* the earth move, too. Sitting by the window in our hotel, playing dominoes with Larry Brown, Kevin Smith, and Thomas Everett, I felt the room get jolted. I looked outside, down on the sidewalk, and the curb was swaying from side to side! I said, "What the . . . WHAT?" When it dawned on me I was sitting next to a window—in a tall, thin building, no less—I jumped out of my chair and ran for the door. My teammates said, "It's an earthquake, it's an earthquake!"

By California standards, it turned out fairly mild, at 5.1. But I'm a Florida boy, and I felt sick to my stomach. Calm down, calm down, calm down, I told myself that night. Just win this game tomorrow and get out of Dodge.

■ ■ ■

As our coaches told us he would, Troy came out throwing. He looked sharp immediately, but so did Steve Young. The first time San Francisco got the ball, Young threw a bomb to Jerry Rice for what looked to be a 63-yard touchdown. Then the refs called one of their offensive linemen for holding. Instead of a 7-point lead, San Francisco had first and 20. Thank you, zebras, thank you.

We got another big call in the second quarter. Losing 7–3, we had third and goal at their 7. We ran a play-action pass, with Troy faking a handoff to me before throwing to somebody else. As I ran through the line pretending to

THE EMMITT ZONE

have the ball, I got tackled by Pierce Holt. At the very same time, Troy was throwing the ball away, since no one was open. It could have been fourth and 7 and time for a field goal, but one of the refs had spotted me getting tackled. That made it first and goal from the two, where I scored a TD to give us a 10–7 lead. The 'Niners then kicked a field goal to make it 10–10 at halftime.

Our first drive the third quarter, we went 78 yards to pull ahead 17–10. It took us only eight plays, because Alvin Harper caught a pass for 38 yards. After their field goal made it 17–13, our next drive was a thing of workmanlike beauty: 79 yards in fourteen plays and nine minutes. Up in the press box, San Francisco's coaches could not predict Norv Turner. Down on the field, Troy kept reading their blitzes and hitting the open man. On one of our key third-down plays, I caught a short pass and got hit by three of their tacklers, but still managed to fight for another first down. Then, on another important third down at their 16, San Francisco made a monumental boo-boo. As Troy dropped back to pass, I drifted to the right flat, expecting to see a linebacker following me. But the linebacker ran left, and Troy hit me, wide open. I scored with ease for my second TD. Dallas 24, San Francisco 13.

After Ken Norton's interception, we moved the ball down to their 7. On fourth and 1, with just seven minutes left, a field goal would put us ahead by 14. Jimmy went for the touchdown anyway—and I made a lousy run. One of their linemen broke through so quickly, he caught me by surprise, and I didn't make a quick enough cut to escape him. I got stopped for no gain and the ball went to San

Francisco. As I ran off the field, I wanted that play back. But I knew it could be a lot worse. We still led San Francisco by 11.

Not for long. Running their hurry-up offense, Young drove them 93 yards in less than three minutes. San Francisco trailed just 24–20, and there was still 4:22 left.

As we started first and 10 from our own 21, I have to admit our huddle seemed anxious. That last drive sent the momentum back to them, and if we went three and out, we knew Steve Young would have plenty of time to beat us. That's when Norv Turner made one of his gutsiest calls, a first-down pass instead of a run.

Alvin Harper slanted in, Troy hit him in stride, cornerback Don Griffin slipped, and Harper raced 70 yards to the San Francisco 9. I ran to the 6, then Troy turned out the lights with a touchdown pass to Kelvin Martin. After winning the NFC title 30–20, we all praised Alvin Harper for making that giant play. But I also couldn't help giving him a jab.

"Hey, Harper," I said. "If you're so fast, how come you didn't score? Why'd you get caught at the nine?"

Alvin laughed and we gave each other a hug. I must have hugged and hooped and hollered for one hour straight. After also having played such a dramatic game, I felt completely drained. Completely drained and wonderful, that is. We were on our way to the Super Bowl.

■　■　■

The week before we played the 49ers, Dallas reporters were talking about an unusual stat. In the history of the NFL, no rushing leader had ever played in the Super Bowl. I

THE EMMITT ZONE

thought it was neat that I would become the first. I also found it baffling. Why hadn't it happened up until now?

That's what the writers wanted to know, but nobody had an answer. Our backfield coach, Joe Brodsky, said, " 'Strange' is a good word for it. It's hard to believe."

"It's just one of those weird things," Norv Turner said. "I don't think there really is a logical explanation."

I didn't see one either, so I simply told the writers, "There's a first time for everything."

That's pretty much my attitude toward life. If we never sell ourselves short, we can make anything happen.

■   ■   ■

Two days after we beat San Francisco, the rumors were confirmed: Dave Wannstedt was leaving next season to coach the Chicago Bears. I was happy for Dave; so were Jimmy Johnson and everyone else on our team. But a selfish part of us all had hoped the rumors were wrong. Unlike some coaches, Wannstedt always wanted to hear what his players were thinking. Mostly he talked to his defensive guys—who loved him, by the way. But if we were playing a team with a dangerous runner, Barry Sanders for example, sometimes Wannstedt would even talk to me. Against this particular defense, he would ask, against this particular blitz, how would I react and where would I go? I thought that was smart. By picking my brain, he was trying to mess with Barry's.

After his press conference in Chicago Monday night, Wannstedt was Wannstedt. He flew straight back to Dallas and took care of business—preparing his defense to play the Buffalo Bills.

EMMITT SMITH

Later that week, I made the cover of *Sports Illustrated* for the first time in my life. With both my arms wrapped around the football and a 49er wrapped around my neck, I was running though a headline that read "EMMITT SMITH LEADS THE COWBOYS TO PASADENA." Steve Young had made the cover the week before, and as well as he played against us, his team got beat. Now the media wanted to know if the *SI* jinx scared me. I said, "No, I'm not concerned. We're off this Sunday, remember? The Super Bowl will not be played until next week."

I didn't add, "Thank God," but that's what I was thinking. As I'll get to later, the following year the jinx really freaked me out.

On Sunday we flew west—straight into one traditional week of Super Bowl hype. In fact, the media itself is now so self-conscious about it, most of the hype that week was about the hype. "This is your first time in the Super Bowl. How do you deal with all the distractions? How do you stay focused amidst all the hoopla?"

Zzzzzz.

Even the media looked bored, and they were asking the questions.

For Michael Irvin, Troy Aikman, and me, the hype-machine got rolling with Magic Johnson. Working for one of the networks, Magic interviewed us at our Loews Hotel in Santa Monica. We all gave our basic Super Bowl rap, then Magic asked what we each hoped to achieve individually. I don't recall what Troy and Mike said, but I told Magic the truth: I wanted to be the Super Bowl MVP. Three or four touchdowns would also be nice, I said.

Magic seemed like an excellent guy, but he wasn't the

only celebrity I met. I also got introduced to Tisha Campbell, Arsenio Hall, John Singleton, Martin Lawrence, and
Wesley Snipes. It wasn't like we were locked up in our hotel
rooms. Though everyone managed to always get back by
curfew, my teammates and I went out almost every night in
L.A. Jimmy knew all about it. His message to us that week:
Don't freeze up because it's the Super Bowl. Stay loose and
enjoy yourselves out here. But don't you dare forget how
much you've gone through to get here.

In case anybody did, Jimmy drove us hard all week in
practice. And every day our practices were crisp. It might
have been our best week of practice all year, a testament
both to our players and to our coaches. Some teams practice poorly before the Super Bowl because they change
their routine. Our practices stayed exactly the same, right
down to the minute. We hadn't come this far to suddenly
rest on our laurels. Even a narrow win wasn't our goal. We
wanted to crush the Bills. We weren't bitter rivals, like we
were with the Eagles, Redskins, Cardinals, and Giants. But
we wanted to make our mark on the NFL; the Bills were
trying to stop us.

■　■　■

The Saturday night before the game, Jimmy moved us to
the Beverly Garland Hotel. He wanted us closer to
Pasadena, where some 98,000 people would pack themselves into the Rose Bowl. That Saturday night at our new
hotel, I was too wired to get much rest. Like a kid the night
before Christmas, I couldn't wait for morning.

I popped out of bed at the wake-up call, ate breakfast

with our whole team, went to an offensive meeting, attended our chapel service, and headed over to the Rose Bowl. As some of the other early birds trickled in, we realized how small our locker room was. I could tell our guys were pretty relaxed, though. Rather than griping, everyone just made jokes.

Why should we be uptight? Because this was our first Super Bowl and Buffalo's third? We didn't see it that way. We definitely respected Buffalo's team. They were here at the Super Bowl again, and twenty-six other ball clubs had not been able to do that. But we were the champs of the NFC, the tougher of the two conferences. We'd just had a great week of practice. And we simply felt that we were the better team.

Finally, no more talking and no more waiting. I was standing in the tunnel, listening to the announcer call out my teammates on offense, when the sheer size of the moment really hit me. Last football game of the year. Twenty-seven friends and family up in the buzzing stands. At home, on the tube, millions of people watching all over the world. As I ran out on the field at the sound of my name, my body started to shake from adrenaline shooting through me. It was time to get after this thing.

The same feeling occurred to the Buffalo Bills. Their defense in particular came out hyped, and our first series on offense netted 1 yard. On fourth and 9, their special-teams whiz Steve Tasker blocked our punt. After Buffalo recovered at our 16, Thurman Thomas scored four plays later. Buffalo 7, Cowboys zip.

Were we worried? No. Too early. And when we went

nowhere again the following series, we kept our cool then too. All season long, it frequently took a few series before our offense ran smoothly. That's usually true on any football team. Defense runs more on emotion, offense on execution.

Going into the game, Jimmy had talked about Buffalo's habit of turning over the ball. Especially against our attacking defense, Jimmy felt it was only a matter of time. It happened first near the end of the first quarter, as James Washington intercepted Jim Kelly. A few plays later, Troy threw a strike to Jay Novacek for a 23-yard TD that tied the game.

From that pass on, Troy had his rhythm the rest of the afternoon. Jim Kelly, meanwhile, seemed a little bit rattled by our defense. The very next series after his interception, Charles Haley sacked him at the 2, Kelly fumbled, and our tackle, Jimmie Jones, ran in for an easy touchdown. With a 14–7 lead at the end of the first quarter, our defense was smelling blood.

Ken Norton then knocked Kelly out of the game. The hit was perfectly clean, but Kelly reinjured a knee he'd hurt in the playoffs. Even though I respect Kelly, I didn't think the game was suddenly ours. Just a few weeks before, when Kelly first hurt his knee, Frank Reich had led the Bills to a stunning 41–38 comeback against the Oilers. The Bills had been losing that game, 38–3. With our own lead only 7, I figured Reich could do the same thing to us.

It had rained in L.A. the night before the game. Sunday morning came up a flawless blue, but the Rose Bowl field was still surprisingly soft and wet. In the second quarter, I felt the slippery grass cost me a touchdown. On a draw trap to the right, I got a perfect block by Nate Newton and made it to the outside. Michael Irvin took out another Bill downfield, and I thought I was gone, but as I cut inside Mike's block, I lost my footing and somebody caught me. In my first big run of the game, I went for 38 yards to their 19-yard line. But I wanted that touchdown badly. I still had my sights on the Super Bowl MVP.

Then Troy Aikman and Michael Irvin made their own bids. One play after I ran for 38 yards, Troy found Michael in one-on-one coverage. Boom, 19-yard touchdown. Troy and Mike hooked up again our next possession, this time from 18 yards out, to put us up 28–10. Troy and Michael, man; put them in the Super Bowl and they think they have to go wild.

In our locker room at halftime, we knew Michael Jackson's show was mesmerizing the crowd, but everyone wanted Michael to wrap it up. With an 18-point lead, we couldn't wait to come back and finish the job.

The second half was all Dallas, especially the fourth quarter. Our lead as the quarter started was 31–17, but then Troy threw a beautiful bomb to Alvin Harper, who turned it into a 45-yard TD. I made a nice block that play on their linebacker, Cornelius Bennett. He was blitzing from the inside, and I popped him in the chest and knocked him off stride. My block accomplished two things: It gave Troy the extra time to find Harper, and it looked good on TV when they showed the replay. Bennett's much bigger than I am, and just about every year he goes to the Pro Bowl.

On our next drive I finally scored my own touchdown.

THE EMMITT ZONE

By then, I had started to think it might not happen. Back in the third quarter, we had driven all the way down to the Buffalo 2. I thought they'd give me the ball, but we ended up passing again. Both frustrated and surprised, I thought: Why the hell are we passing from the 2-yard line? Looking back on it now, they probably wanted Troy to get the record for Super Bowl touchdown passes.

My own TD came on third and goal from the ten. Norv Turner called the draw play, I broke a few tackles, and I barreled into the end zone. The moment I crossed the goal line, I felt all my frustration fade away. I felt all pumped up, in fact. I knew how many good running backs never played in the Super Bowl. I knew Walter Payton, one of the greatest, did play in one Super Bowl, but he never got to score. Now I'd played in the Super Bowl *and* scored a touchdown!

My TD made it 45–17. Ken Norton closed out the scoring by running back a fumble, and then came the unforgettable Leon Lett play.

First let me set the stage, because most people don't know this part of the story. Remember that play in the first quarter, when Charles Haley forced Jim Kelly to fumble and our tackle Jimmie Jones ran it in for a touchdown? Later on, in the second half, I was standing next to Leon Lett on our sideline.

Leon said, "Dawg! Jimmie Jones stole my touchdown! I should've had that one!"

I said, "You're still talking about that play? Stop whining, man. Why don't you get back out there and make a play? Go get your own fumble and take it in for a touchdown."

EMMITT SMITH

Only one or two series later, Leon got his big chance. Scooping up a Frank Reich fumble, he went rumbling down the sideline for an apparent 64-yard touchdown. Except that Leon started to hotdog before he crossed the goal line. Holding the football in one outstretched hand for the world to see, Leon let Don Beebe catch him from behind. Beebe slapped the ball away just before Leon scored. It flew out of the end zone and Buffalo got a touchback.

The game already a rout, I was laughing when Leon came off the field. I said to him, "See? You *had* a touchdown. But you wanted to showboat bcforc you got into the end zone. You blew it, Leon."

He said, "Yeah, man, I know!"

Leon was laughing too, but I could tell he was deeply embarrassed. At least this time the game was already decided, so the media didn't come down too hard on him. When Leon made that mistake the next year against Miami, the fallout was much more ugly. But we can get to that later.

Shortly before the game ended at 52–17, it was announced that Troy had won Super Bowl MVP. Mike Irvin and I had good numbers, too. Mike caught 6 passes for 114 yards and a pair of touchdowns. To go with my touchdown, I gained 108 yards on 22 carries, and I caught 6 passes for 27 yards more. As the Bills kept sending in linebackers on blitzes, I also threw several good blocks. Still, it's hard to compete with a guy who goes 22 of 30 for 273 yards and 4 TDs. Without a doubt, Troy deserved to be Super Bowl MVP. Furthermore, that Sunday just capped off a roll he'd been on since the playoffs started. In our

THE EMMITT ZONE

wins over the Bills, 49ers, and Eagles, Troy threw 8 touchdown passes without even one interception.

But you know who else deserved an award? Our entire defensive unit. Not just for causing a Super Bowl–record 9 turnovers, but for playing the best defense in the NFL that whole season. "Defense wins championships," Jimmy Johnson has always preached. Even yours truly, an offensive player, feels that way.

Speaking of Jimmy, it was now the moment we'd waited for all year: the messing up of his hair. As our victory celebration began along our sideline, Nate Newton and Charles Haley took the first shot. They dumped our cooler on him, but I swear Jimmy's hair never moved one strand. If anything, it got harder. So I hollered, "Mess it up! Mess up his hair!" When nobody did, I took it upon myself. Even Jimmy was laughing as I worked over his hair. At that moment in his life, nobody could deny the magic he had performed: He'd taken the Dallas Cowboys from 1–15 to Super Bowl champs in four years.

Jimmy got emotional in our postgame locker room. He told us before the media arrived: "The feeling you have at this very moment is one of the best things you will ever have in life, especially the feeling you have for each other. That's even more important than the winning itself—the feeling of accomplishment with your teammates."

I really liked what Jimmy said, but he left something out: The feeling we had for our coach at that very moment.

EMMITT SMITH

13
CONTRACT DISPUTE

After the Pro Bowl in Honolulu the first week of February, I went back to Pensacola to get some rest. Still a few months shy of twenty-four, I had just finished my third NFL season. These were a few of the facts of my career so far:

After forty-eight regular-season games, I had 4,213 yards. Among all running backs in NFL history, only Eric Dickerson, Jim Brown, and Walter Payton had rushed for more yardage at that same stage.

In leading the league in rushing two years in a row, I had gained 1,563 yards in 1991 and 1,713 in 1992. I had also scored 30 touchdowns those two seasons.

I had played in three straight Pro Bowls.

I was the first player ever to win the rushing championship and the Super Bowl in the same season, and the first Cowboy to run for 100 yards in a Super Bowl.

Games in which I carried twenty times or more, the Dallas Cowboys were 29–1. We were 21–1 when I rushed for 100 yards.

And I still hadn't missed a game in the course of my career.

Pretty good numbers, right? So where was I that February, financially speaking? Having just completed the terms of my first pro contract, my base salary the previous year had been about $465,000. And even with incentives that I earned, I still made less than $750,000. That simply wasn't a lot for an NFL rushing leader.

That's how it goes sometimes. I signed that deal as a rookie, before I'd proven myself in the NFL. Once I showed what I could do, I asked for a contract extension, and Jerry told me to wait. When he finally made an unsatisfactory offer, I still didn't press the issue. I just kept performing.

Well, now my contract was up, and I wanted my true value in the market.

Sitting down with my agent early that March, I told Richard I wanted to be the highest-paid nonquarterback in pro football. I'd probably never get quarterback money, I knew; those guys are in another dimension.

Just because I knew this, even accepted it, didn't mean I thought it made any sense. Quarterback obviously is a very important position. But there are quarterbacks in this league who don't excel, whose teams don't normally win, and they still earn $3 or $4 million a year. Then there are

EMMITT SMITH

premier players at other positions, players helping their teams get into the playoffs, who still aren't close to $3 or $4 million a year. That's the system, I know. But is that system fair?

Anyway, I told myself that winter: "Forget about quarterback money. Out of the rest of the guys in this league, who's the highest paid?"

That brought me to Reggie White, the former Eagle, who'd just signed with the Packers for $17 million over four years. Based on my own worth to the Cowboys, I wanted that much or more: four years at $17 million. Actually, the part about the four years was Jerry's idea. Once Jerry wanted to tie me up for that long—while refusing to put in any escalator clause—I arrived at the sum of $17 million.

I realize that's an awful lot of money. So was what I eventually signed for. But whether a person plays pro football, works at a record store, fixes cars, or delivers the mail, he or she wants to be paid the going rate in that business. Especially if they do a good job every day.

That winter, we didn't go right to Jerry with what we wanted. At that early stage, we wanted to keep our options open, by talking to other teams. As part of the new collective bargaining agreement, I had just been designated a "restricted free agent." This didn't mean I could just sign with any team that came courting. That's an "*un*restricted free agent," as in Reggie White. As a restricted free agent, I had the right to negotiate with other teams, but the Cowboys had the right to match any offer I got. If they did, I'd be obligated to stay with them.

From February to about the first week of April, my

agent contacted teams from his office in Atlanta. Before he started, I told him I was most open to Miami, Phoenix, and Atlanta. In Miami, I felt I could slow the pass rush on Dan Marino, punch up their running game, and help them into the Super Bowl. I liked the weather in Phoenix, the players were young, and the team seemed to be moving in the right direction. Since it would mean I could be close to my family, Atlanta's location was appealing. I also enjoy the energy in Atlanta, and I *love* the Georgia Dome. That building is magnificent. Congratulations, Atlanta: It's the finest football facility I've ever seen.

So what happened that winter? Nothing. Not one team in the league made me an offer. Think about that for a moment. Two-time NFL rushing leader, age twenty-three, dedicated player who stays out of trouble, significant part of a Super Bowl champion team—and nobody can use him?

That didn't smell quite right. Then my agent and I began hearing rumors: Jerry was telling his fellow owners not to waste their time, because he would match any offer they put on the table.

Another scenario also occurred to me. If Reggie White got $17 million as an unrestricted free agent, then I got $18 million even though I was restricted, another restricted free agent, like Barry Sanders, might end up with $20 million. That could have a ripple effect throughout the league.

In any case, it definitely helped Jerry when I didn't get any offers. Without any competition from his peers, he could just sit back and play his usual waiting game.

By March I'd returned from Pensacola to Dallas. By the end of May, with training camp six weeks away, we still didn't have an offer from the Cowboys. To get this process rolling, my agent and I decided we needed to go to them.

Our first meeting, in June, wasn't too bad. With each side still feeling the other out, Jerry never made any offer, and we didn't tell him exactly what we wanted. Jerry did mention the NFL salary cap, which would not kick in until the following season, but which Jerry was using right now as a reason he couldn't pay me.

Frankly, I didn't buy it. The Cowboys at the time were reportedly the twenty-fourth lowest-paid team in the NFL. Even if Jerry paid his players more freely, I figured he'd only move up to the middle of the pack. Also, the salary cap didn't start until February of 1994. By front-loading my new contract, paying me a large portion in 1993, that money wouldn't count against next year's cap. Then Jerry would have three years to disburse the balance. My bottom-line feeling: He could work around the cap if he wanted to.

At our first meeting, Jerry also said something along the lines of, "You're lucky to be a Dallas Cowboy. This is America's Team. Everyone wants that association. You should be proud to be part of America's Team."

I was waiting for John Wayne to come riding into his office. Jerry made it sound like it was my patriotic duty to sign with the Dallas Cowboys. He made it sound like I should pay them. The heck with my performance since I came into this league, with the beating I took every Sunday, with the average career of NFL players, which is only three or four years, meaning we have limited time to make our living from football. The way Jerry talked, I should kiss

THE EMMITT ZONE

the ground and thank my lucky stars that I played for America's Team.

So far, Jerry had done most of the talking. But at least the meeting was friendly, and he really hadn't said anything unexpected. Then, toward the end, as almost a parting shot, Jerry said, "You know something, Emmitt? I'd walk across Texas for five dollars."

He seemed to be saying: "Damn right I'm tight, and proud of it, too."

That set off some alarm bells.

Still, I wanted the meeting to end on an optimistic note. So I told Jerry just before we left, "I know this could be a long process, but we don't have to make it one. If we can get this started right away, I can be here for training camp. And it doesn't have to get played out in the press, like it did when I was a rookie. None of us need that hoopla again."

Jerry agreed. He also said, "I promise you, we're not gonna blast your people like we did the first time."

All in all, I felt pretty good when I left. And so straight from Jerry's office, I went to one of our summer workouts. In the month of June I attended them all, even though I had no contract or even an offer. At that point, I thought Jerry might mean what he said about doing this quickly.

On the other hand, if Jerry really did plan on dragging this out, my agent and I also weighed other possibilities. If Jerry's offer came in and it was lousy, we talked about seeking a trade. Or else maybe I'd go back to college, sit out this NFL season, and see what teams came after me the next year. But this was just talk between a player and agent, and nothing we shared with anyone else. My first choice was still to stay with my teammates and Jimmy Johnson.

EMMITT SMITH

The Cowboys presented an offer in early July. As in my rookie year, their numbers and our numbers weren't even close. The Cowboys offered $9 million for four or five years. If they wanted me for that long, we said, then let's make it four years at $17 million. As *Sports Illustrated* observed, the gap was "about as wide as the Lone Star State."

There was no movement on either side the week before training camp. By NFL regulations, a player can't attend camp without a signed contract. So once it began on July 15, I went back to Pensacola and worked out there. Some days I ran hills. Some days I sprinted on the track at Escambia High. I stayed in touch with my teammates during this time, and they kept me informed on two fronts: how we looked on offense and defense at training camp, and what was being said in the Dallas media. But a week or so into camp, I could monitor things right there in Pensacola. My contract dispute was becoming national news.

Face-to-face, in the street, most people in Pensacola were very encouraging. They figured to be—I grew up there. But so were the people I met when I traveled to other cities. A few people said, "You need to get back down there and play some football." But many more told me, "Go and get paid, go get your money. You deserve what you're asking for." Even most of the media seemed to be siding with me. I appreciated that. Some of the media don't like to upset the NFL establishment; it's much easier pointing the finger at "greedy modern athletes." This time, I felt the media was more objective.

In the first week or so of August, after one of the Cowboys' preseason games, Jimmy got on our running backs in the newspapers. There were some fumbles, some performances he didn't like. Later that week, I heard the Cowboys might trade me for Cleveland Gary. I didn't believe it, though. I thought Jerry Jones planted a seed in the Dallas press, so he could put pressure on me. Cleveland Gary is known for running hard, but I couldn't see him playing for Jimmy Johnson.

In our meeting back in June, Jerry had promised not to publicly blast my agent. To his credit, Jerry largely kept that promise. As for keeping this thing quiet, not splashing it all over the newspapers and TV, Jerry sang like a hummingbird.

He said, "Emmitt Smith is a luxury, not a necessity, for the Cowboys."

He said, "The Cowboys can win a Super Bowl without Emmitt Smith."

I thought: No, that isn't true. The Cowboys are good, but I have to be there. You underestimate my value to this team. You also underestimate my resolve.

That's how I felt, but I kept those feelings private. Even when Jerry started blabbing, I barely spoke to the press. The few times I did, I kept my comments restrained. That's *my* style, and I won't let anyone else's behavior change it.

As the clock kept ticking ahead toward the regular season, somebody told me that Jimmy tried getting involved. When I was a rookie, I was told, Jimmy had influenced Jerry to finally sign me. But when Jimmy tried now, as I understood it, Jerry basically told him to stay out of it, that this had nothing to do with him.

In a sense, though, it did. Jimmy was trying to win another Super Bowl. He wanted his starting tailback.

EMMITT SMITH

A few weeks earlier, Thurman Thomas had signed a new contract with the Bills. He signed for $13.5 over four years, and his contract was not even up yet. The Bills gave Thurman Thomas an extension, because they felt he deserved it. And yet, with the regular season a few weeks away, Jerry Jones was still at $9 million, or $4.5 million less than "Thurman Thomas money." This was the phrase that was getting used by the press, but I actually didn't want what Thurman was getting. I still wanted to be the highest-paid nonquarterback in the league. Jerry, evidently, did not even want me to be the highest-paid running back.

With his offer stuck at four or five years for $9 million, Jerry seemed to feel no urgency at all. Sometimes he and his people seemed to be stalling on purpose. When my agent contacted their office, they'd sometimes return his phone call at weird hours, hours when they must have known he wouldn't be there.

Back in Pensacola, I was getting concerned, but I wasn't a bundle of nerves. I kept running hills and sprints, playing some golf, working at Emmitt, Inc., my store in Pensacola. My family and I sell football cards, sports apparel, and various items of sports memorabilia for sports fans. People can walk in our store or order by mail. I enjoy this part of my life, and I work hard at it, too. I want to be a great athlete and a great businessman.

Around the final week of August, the Cowboys called us. But things weren't looking too promising. They only called; they didn't increase their original offer. If they still wanted $9 million, we told them we'd probably do it, but only for two years.

THE EMMITT ZONE

The Cowboys said no.

When we proposed a one-year deal at $3.5 million, they turned this down too. I can't say I was surprised. If I signed for one year, the next year I would become an unrestricted free agent. Then the Cowboys might lose me forever.

Back in Dallas, some of my teammates were standing up for me. Michael Irvin was popping off all over. "We need to get Emmitt in here," he said in print and on TV. "How can we be the same team if we don't have all our weapons?"

Nate Newton and Troy Aikman also came out in public. It made me feel good, but I still had no idea how this would all turn out. With the regular season ten days away, I figured Jerry would stretch me out until the last minute, then come in with a serious offer once he saw he couldn't bluff me. But if Jerry stayed where he was, I was also prepared to sit out the entire season. I would go back to Gainesville and start earning the last eighteen credits toward my degree.

The *Dallas Morning News* put the question to the community—or to part of the community, in my view. In a poll they published August 29, 51 percent of those polled supported Jerry Jones, 35 percent supported me, and 13 percent were undecided. I thought that was funny. What neighborhoods did they canvass? Did they go to south Dallas, ask the black people there to vote? Nah, I didn't believe that poll. In my opinion, it was culturally biased.

I guess I've opened a can of worms. You're probably thinking: Forget about that poll. Did Emmitt feel his contract dispute was even partly racial? Do white players, in general, get treated better financially than black players?

Those are hard questions, without any simple answers. But I'll talk about it anyway, later on, when we get to the regular season—December, to be exact, when Troy Aikman signed his contract for $50 million. That's right: $50 million. I couldn't believe it either. My jaw dropped so low it landed on my carpet.

About a week before our first game with the Redskins, Jerry upped his offer to roughly $10 million. That wasn't peanuts. It also wasn't enough. Thurman Thomas, as I said, signed for $13.5 million in July. I wanted that much at least now. Hell, I thought Jerry should have started off there. But he'd stayed at $9 million for weeks, then finally bettered his offer by only $1 million. And that was still over four or five years.

We told the Cowboys no.

Regardless, I still had hope those last few days. I figured they'd call on Sunday with something decent, I'd fly to Washington that night, and then I'd play against the Redskins on *Monday Night Football*.

It didn't happen that way. Sunday came and went without a new offer. So did Monday morning and afternoon. As I sat down to watch the Monday night game, I couldn't believe this was happening. Perfectly healthy, twenty-four years old, in the prime of my career or maybe not even there yet, I was at home watching my teammates go to battle without me. A part of me even felt I was letting them down. They were about to play the Redskins at RFK, and I was still fighting with Jerry Jones about money.

Derrick Lassic, a rookie from Alabama, was starting in place of me. When I met him at our precamp workouts, I liked him immediately. With all the scrutiny Derrick was under now, I wanted him to play well against the Redskins. And I absolutely wanted my teammates to win. I knew I'd lose leverage with Jerry, but I didn't care.

As the Washington fans ate it up, the Redskins whipped us 35–16. On offense we turned the ball over three times. For the first time since the Cowboys went 1–15, our defense allowed five touchdowns. It was a bad night all around, and I woke up Tuesday feeling tremendous frustration. We already had one loss, with a Super Bowl rematch on Sunday against the Bills. Still, I was not about to move. I wasn't asking Jerry for the damn moon. Quarterbacks get the moon; running backs don't. I just wanted something fair.

Richard Howell called me that week. The Cowboys had upped their offer to roughly $12 million. I turned it down, thinking: Jerry's still playing games. We've told him ten times I won't sign for that.

I was so fed up by then, my feeling was getting stronger. Even if Buffalo beat us Sunday, I wouldn't take Jerry's offer. There was a stubbornness setting in on my part now.

Everything changed for me that Sunday, September 12. While I watched the game on TV with a friend in Tallahassee, the Bills won 13–10 at Texas Stadium. This week the defense played well, especially in the fourth quarter, when they allowed the Bills to gain only 14 yards. But the offense looked tight and kept turning over the ball. All 13 of Buffalo's points came after Dallas mistakes.

With twelve seconds left and losing 13–10, the Cowboys had a chance to win or tie anyway. They drove to a second and 4 at the Buffalo 11, and the only question seemed to be touchdown or field goal? But then Troy missed Jay Novacek over the middle, Buffalo intercepted, and the Bills ran out the clock. It shocked me when our guys lost. I thought for sure they would pull it out.

Before leaving Tallahassee for Pensacola, I turned on ESPN for the postgame press conference. Jimmy was so upset he almost couldn't speak. When I say upset, I don't mean angry. Jimmy looked shaken and vulnerable, and I'd never seen him this way. Seeing that shook me up.

On the drive back to Pensacola Sunday evening, I replayed it all in my mind. The stunned look on Jimmy's face on national TV, the loss to the Bills, the entire contract dispute. I thought: Maybe I better go in, get the best I can, and go on about my business. Later, when my next contract is done, I'll think hard about whether to stay with the Dallas Cowboys.

In Pensacola that night, I found out what happened with Charles Haley and Derrick Lassic. Derrick had fumbled twice, one of them leading to 3 points for the Bills. In the locker room after the game, Charles Haley slammed his helmet into a wall. Then, while walking near Derrick's locker, Charles yelled: "We're never going to win with this rookie running back!"

When I heard that, I felt even more compelled to get myself back in uniform. A veteran player on defense had screamed at a rookie on offense. It sounded to me like our locker room was dividing.

Richard Howell called me that Sunday night at my parents' house. We talked about the Buffalo game, the leverage it probably cost Jerry, what might happen this upcoming week. Normally cool, Richard sounded intense.

"If we don't get it done this week," he said, "it might not happen this year."

I figured Richard was right. If Jerry didn't move now after two straight losses, with his locker room in disarray, I thought I'd miss the entire season.

In the story about the Cowboys-Bills game that week in *Sports Illustrated*, Jimmy Johnson was asked how he felt about the standoff. "I know this about Emmitt Smith," Jimmy said. "He's a very proud player who won't back down from anyone on the field. And he won't back down in this thing, either."

Finally, after two losses, Jerry came to the place where I felt we should have started—$13.5 million. But the deal was back-end-loaded, and I declined. I also told Richard, "I want to talk to Jerry myself." Up until then, I'd felt Richard and Jerry should do the negotiating. I knew how heated these things can get, and I'm not one to take personal statements lightly, even when they're made in the name of "business."

Now, after watching my teammates and friends lose their first two games, I felt we needed another approach. I wanted Jerry to understand, loud and clear, that I was the one who was asking for this money. Sometimes owners think agents are calling the shots, so they can receive a higher commission. I also wanted to hear *exactly* what Jerry was saying. My trust in Richard wasn't the issue; he had that completely. But this was my future being decided, not Richard's or Jerry's.

Richard agreed. We held a conference call on Wednesday, with Jerry Jones in New York, his son and Cowboy vice president Stephen Jones in Dallas, Richard Howell in Atlanta, and myself in Pensacola.

Jerry Jones did most of the talking again. When I tried speaking, sometimes he acted like he couldn't hear me. I'd make a point, he'd say he couldn't hear me, then he'd change the subject right away. One time, out of the blue, Jerry said, "I understand you haven't picked up your Super Bowl ring."

What in the world is this? I thought.

Jerry said, "How would you like it if we FedExed it to you?"

I said, "No, Jerry, how does this sound? How about if I pick it up when I come to Dallas? To clean out my locker."

"What was that, Stephen?" Jerry said to his son. "Stephen, did you hear what Emmitt said?"

This went on in a similar vein. Then Jerry said toward the end of the conversation: "This is the best I can do. That's all there is to it."

"I *know* this isn't the best you can do," I said. "How would you feel if I told you the best I could do was sixty yards a game?"

We said good-bye and hung up with nothing resolved. But I felt good about this thing now, better than I had in weeks. Jerry's attitude, and tone, confirmed my feeling that I had been doing right.

On Thursday morning I flew to Atlanta, where Richard Howell picked me up at the airport. "I have some news for you," Richard said. "The Cowboys upped their offer."

I said, "Oh really?"

He said, "Yes, and I think you'll like this one."

It was four years at $13.6 million, including a $4 million signing bonus ($1 million of it deferred until 1994), and a salary that first season of $3 million. This front-loaded part of the deal was the turning point for me. Since Jerry wouldn't give me a guaranteed contract, I would stop being paid if an injury cut my career short. So the money up-front was meaningful to me.

We never even ate lunch. First Richard called the Cowboys and took the deal. Then, from Dallas, they dispatched Jerry's private plane to pick us up in Atlanta. By coincidence, Jerry was flying into Atlanta on a commercial flight from New York. Just one big happy family, we could all fly back to Dallas on Jerry's plane.

With Richard sitting in back, shutting his mouth, Jerry and I were still negotiating. Actually, I was negotiating. Jerry, to my astonishment, seemed to imply that he stood to make a killing since buying the Cowboys. I was just looking at him, wondering, How can you be saying this to me, after what we've been through?

As Jerry kept talking, I thought, The man makes me look greedy in the press, then brags to my face?

Still, in light of all that had happened, our flight back to Dallas was relatively pleasant. Then Jerry Jones blew me away again that night. At the press conference we called at Texas Stadium, with the club lounge packed with photographers and reporters, Jerry acted like I stole the money from him. I'm not lying; it felt like a funeral in there. That afternoon on his plane, Jerry had been talking a mile a minute. That night he spoke slowly, gravely, about "winners" and "losers" in contract disputes like this.

And then it only got worse. When it came time for Jerry to hand me my signing bonus, he looked like he'd rather drink poison.

I couldn't believe it. He still didn't seem to want me to have that check.

The good news was, this three-ring circus was over and there was work to be done. No team had ever lost the first two games of its season, then won a Super Bowl. No running back had ever missed two games in a season and gone on to win a rushing title.

It was time to prove things again.

14
BACK IN THE SADDLE

O n Saturday morning, two days after I signed, I flew with my teammates to Phoenix to play the Cardinals. It felt great to be back, and those guys seemed glad to see me. Nobody even talked about what happened. It was almost like the season had been postponed and now it was starting for real, and everyone was excited.

■ ■ ■

Before leaving Dallas, Jimmy had asked if I wanted to start against Phoenix.

"No, I think Lassic should start," I said.

"Let's talk about it on Sunday," Jimmy said. "I'll make my decision then."

For a couple reasons, I thought Lassic should start. After practicing all week to play the Cardinals, he deserved to. Also, my hamstring had tightened one day while I was working out on the track at Escambia High. I'd cut back on my running after that, but the muscle still felt sore when I returned to the Cowboys. I didn't want to rush it, maybe complicate the damage.

Sunday night in Phoenix was warm and clear—a perfect night for football. I knew I might not see a lot of action, though. Jimmy told me before the game, "We're going with Lassic. I don't want you going out there and trying to do too much, and end up pulling that hamstring."

"That's fine with me," I said.

"If we need you, I'll just put you in," Jimmy said.

They really didn't need me. On 14 carries, Lassic gained 60 yards and scored 2 touchdowns. When Jimmy put me in in the third quarter, just to give me some work, we had a 17–0 lead.

By that point I couldn't wait to get out there. Missing our first two games only made me hungrier. I considered myself the best running back in football. I thought I was worth every penny I got and then some. Starting tonight, I wanted to show this to everyone else.

I gained 45 yards on 8 carries, for a 5.6-yard average. We beat Phoenix 17–10 for our first win of the year. At 1–2, we were two games behind the Giants and Eagles in the NFC East.

In our home opener against Green Bay, Jimmy put me

back in the starting lineup, but I aggravated my hamstring on a toss right. The blocking was so perfect, I scored a 22-yard TD without even running full speed. That was what worried me. What would happen when I started going full throttle?

Still, I ended up with 71 yards on only 13 carries. Troy completed 18 of 23 passes for 317 yards. Michael Irvin exploded for 155 yards on 7 receptions, and Alvin Harper caught 2 passes for 80. In his first season as a Cowboy, Eddie Murray hit 5 of 5 field goals, including one from 50 yards and another from 48. From that performance on, we called him Eddie Money.

It was a great Sunday afternoon at Texas Stadium. After all the dissension that had started this season, we blew out the Packers 38–14. Up until then, we'd only scored 43 points in our first three games.

That evened our record at 2–2, with Indianapolis next at the Hoosier Dome. This week the real star was our defense. Thomas Everett intercepted Jack Trudeau twice, Kevin Smith and Ken Norton, Jr., had an interception each, and we overpowered the Colts 27–3.

Despite the cold weather in Indianapolis, my hamstring felt loose for the first time that season. On 25 carries, I rushed for 104 yards and scored a 20-yard touchdown. It was my first 100-yard game, and that felt nice. But what made me feel best that day was a simple pass I caught out in the flat. As I turned upfield, I saw a cornerback racing at me from the right and a linebacker closing from the left. I kept running straight ahead, until they were about to crunch me from either side. Just before they did, I stopped

THE EMMITT ZONE

and spun and they ended up smashing each other. I only gained 13 yards, but that wasn't the point. The play was sweet; it told me I was ready.

Keeping their watch on the NFL, *Sports Illustrated* may have sensed the same thing. They called me a few days later when I returned to Dallas. Five games into the season, I trailed Barry Sanders by 313 yards in the rushing-leader race. What with my having missed our first two and a half games, the guy from *SI* asked me to assess my chances.

"I need to have a couple really huge days to get back in the race," I said. "I look at it this way: No one ever won a rushing title and the Super Bowl in the same season until I did it last year. If there's anyone in the NFL who can do it, I think I'm the man."

On October 17, in a rematch of the past season's NFC Championship Game, we played the 49ers at Texas Stadium. With three straight wins—the last two by a combined score of 65–17—we felt confident we could beat them. But we also knew San Francisco would come into Dallas psyched. We were the jokers who'd kept them from reaching the Super Bowl.

As usual when we play San Francisco, the pregame hype centered on the offensive "duels." Jerry Rice and Mike Irvin. Steve Young and Troy Aikman. Tom Rathman and Daryl Johnston. Jay Novacek and Brent Jones. Ricky Watters and myself. The fans seem to like this stuff, and I don't know any football players who mind it. I also don't know any who take it seriously. When we prepare for another team, we focus on the guys on the other side of the ball.

On the game's first possession, I got totally used by

their linebacker, John Johnson. After taking a handoff from Troy, I did something I rarely do: I ran east and west. But I wanted to see if I could turn the corner, maybe get something big. John Johnson was running behind me, herding me to the sideline, when he stripped the ball from my hand. Their cornerback, Eric Davis, picked it up on the run, then went 47 yards to put us down 7–0. For the first time in my career, one of my carries had turned into another team's touchdown.

I came back to gain 92 yards and score a touchdown, but even that was a struggle. Determined to stop the run, the 49ers came out in an eight-man front. But as I've said before, against the Cowboys you have to choose your poison. With the 49ers crowding the line of scrimmage, Michael Irvin had single coverage. That's like giving him the key to the vault.

Of Mike's career-high 12 passes for 168 yards, 10 went for first downs. With just more than two minutes left in the third quarter, and the 49ers leading 17–16, he also caught a 36-yard TD pass. We went on to win our fourth straight, 26–17.

With our entire division taking its bye week, the NFC East standings looked like this: Giants, 5–1; Cowboys and Eagles, 4–2; Cardinals, 2–4; Redskins, 1–5. So if we could defeat the Eagles at Veterans Stadium, and the Jets could beat the Giants the same afternoon, we'd tie the Giants for first in the NFC East. Not bad for a club that started out 0–2.

On October 31, heavy rain was falling on Philadelphia. That didn't faze me at all. As a runner, I almost consider the rain to be an advantage. I slip and slide just like the defense, but I know where I'm going and those guys don't. I had also played several high school games in the rain. On a few rainy nights in Pensacola, I had rushed for 300 yards.

It was still pouring at the Vet by kickoff time, so I knew I'd be getting the football that afternoon. The wetter the weather, the harder it is to pass. Finding it hard to grip the ball, Troy would manage just 9 completions for 96 yards.

But man oh man, what a wonderful afternoon it turned into for me. In my best game as a pro, I rushed 30 times for 237 yards. I had ten gains of 8 yards or more. Eight of those ten came in the opening half, when I had more than 100 yards with seven minutes to go before intermission. If not for one play in the first quarter, I'd have probably had about forty more yards, too. Eric Allen reached out and grabbed me in the open field, held on to the back of my jersey, and kept me from breaking a long one for 60 or 70 yards. If Eric weren't so speedy, I'd have gone over 300 yards.

Other than that play, and the time I ran into the back of Alvin Harper, I had no complaints with my performance. As for our blocking, it was fantastic. No matter what blitzes or fronts the Eagles threw us at, we were always able to get a blocker on them. And along with the game ball the coaching staff gave me, Nate Newton and Mark Tuinei each got awarded one too.

Somebody asked me after this game, "Were you in a zone?"

In a manner of speaking, I was. Since it's a feeling, and not a thought, it's hard to describe. But I'll try to, anyway.

EMMITT SMITH

That rainy day against the Eagles, I was just out there *doing:* letting my instincts and feelings tell me which way to run, rather than thinking too much about everything. And I felt so hot and smooth, so natural and unforced, I believed that I could score on any play. If you're an athlete now, or if you ever played ball, at any level, at any age, you know the feeling I mean. And if you haven't gotten it yet, believe me, it will come. And when it does there probably won't be any warning. Because you know what I truly believe? When our special moments come, no matter what shape they take, they're a gift from God. It's almost as if He is saying, "This one is for you; all things are possible. *Now make the best of it.*" That's what the Emmitt Zone is all about.

■ ■ ■

At first, with an early 10–0 lead, it looked like we might blow them out. The Eagles hung tough at home, though. With four minutes left in the game, we had the ball and a 16–10 lead, but the outcome was still very much in doubt. If we punted—or fumbled the ball—the Eagles still had plenty of time to beat us.

On first and 10 from our 32, I gained 6 yards on my twenty-ninth carry. With second and 4, the Eagles came out in a risky ten-man front. But they knew we would be running, and they couldn't afford to let us get a first down. They might not get the ball back if they did.

Norv Turner called a lead draw left. As Troy called out signals before the ball was snapped, one of our wideouts went in motion toward the sideline. I saw the Eagles' free safety following him, leaving center field wide open. I thought, Get through the line of scrimmage and you're gone.

It happened just that way. The Eagles came hard to try to get penetration. Moose, Mark Stepnoski, and Kevin Gogan opened a hole. As I broke into the clear, my only concern was Eric Allen. But this time I knew he was coming. As Eric dove at me from behind, I cut to the side and made him miss. I went all the way in, untouched, for a 62-yard touchdown. That sealed the win for us, 23–10.

In the next few days I heard about all the statistics. With my 237 yards, I had posted the best rushing day in Dallas Cowboys history, surpassing Tony Dorsett's mark of 206. I had gained the most yards in a single NFL game in sixteen years, since Walter Payton had 275 against Minnesota. And I had tied Jim Brown for the sixth-highest rushing day in NFL history. I've told you how much I respect Dorsett and Payton. As for Jim Brown, I've only seen him on film, but I've seen him on *much* film. Jim Brown looked fast in the open field. He looked powerful running through tackles. Most of all, he looked like a player who wouldn't take no for an answer.

It was kind of funny: My name was mentioned that week with three of the all-time greats. I also won NFC Offensive Player of the Week. But I didn't get a game ball from ESPN. For the best performance each week in the NFL, ESPN awards a mythical game ball. Yet they didn't choose me that Sunday against the Eagles, and they didn't pick Michael Irvin the time he went off against Phoenix for 210 yards. Does ESPN have something against the Cowboys? That couldn't be possible, could it? Everyone knows what a lovable group we are.

With 549 yards after seven games, I was also right back in the NFL rushing race. I trailed Barry Sanders by only 241, and Barry still had a bye week coming up. So did Thurman Thomas, Erric Pegram, and Ricky Watters. Of the five runners ahead of me, only Barry Foster had as many games left as I did.

The other detail I liked was our number of carries. Those guys had 181, 166, 134, 147, and 127. Since I had just 103, I felt I could possibly catch them by week thirteen or fourteen.

In beating the Giants at home, 31–9, we moved alone to the top of the NFC East. But trouble struck in the third quarter, when Troy heard his hamstring pop while dodging one of the Giants. With Steve Beuerlein having been signed by the Phoenix Cardinals, Jason Garrett was our backup quarterback now. Jason came in and did a nice job, completing 5 of 6 passes and leading two scoring drives that I capped off with touchdowns. Still, we were concerned when Troy went out. In winning six straight games, we'd also been playing the best football in the league. Troy was a major factor. Now he was out for probably two weeks.

Jimmy Johnson moved quickly. The Monday morning after Troy got injured, Bernie Kosar was cut by the Cleveland Browns. By Wednesday morning, Kosar had signed a contract with the Cowboys.

Jimmy had coached Kosar for one year at Miami, so I wasn't surprised when we picked him up. What did surprise me was the Browns' letting him go. From my impres-

THE EMMITT ZONE

sions of Kosar, he still had a strong arm and a quick release. He still had the art of deception—looking the defense one way, then throwing the ball somewhere else. So why did the Browns release Kosar, a solid player and person and longtime hero in Cleveland? There was talk around the league of a personality conflict between Kosar and Cleveland coach Bill Belichick. For someone like Kosar to be released, that sounded to me like a pretty slim reason. On the other hand, this business is as political as any. Strange things are known to happen, and not only here in Dallas.

Anyway, we were just happy to get the guy. We were even happier once we saw him at practice. What Kosar accomplished that week was truly impressive. Though he had to learn all new plays and terminology, he already seemed to be getting the grasp. Everyone said that Bernie Kosar was smart. Everyone was right.

He also looked good on Sunday against the Cardinals. Entering the game in the first quarter, he completed 13 of 21 passes with no interceptions and 1 TD pass. On his first drive as a Cowboy, our offense went 65 yards on nine plays for a 10–0 lead. On our series after that, I snuck through the line of scrimmage without the ball. Kosar hit me underneath the linebackers, I broke three tackles, and then I raced 85 yards downfield to the Phoenix 1. From there, Kosar and Jay Novacek made it 17–0. Phoenix came back in the second half, but we still held on to win 20–15.

For the first time in ten years, the Dallas Cowboys had won seven straight. The last time we'd lost, against the Bills, I was still back in Pensacola. Now our record was 7–2, Troy was coming back soon, people were calling us the best team in football, and our next game was at Atlanta, where the Falcons were 3–6, with the worst defense in the league. And the last time we played, we had pulverized the Falcons, 41–17.

Somehow, Jimmy Johnson knew this game would be radically different. "I'm expecting a dogfight, guys," he told us that week at practice. "We have to go down there and play our tails off. If we can win thirteen to ten, then I'll be happy."

Our players looked at each other like: Wait a minute. Does this guy know something the rest of us don't?

Because this wasn't like Jimmy Johnson at all. He normally talked about beating people's eyes out. Furthermore, we really didn't think we were getting big heads. We thought we were ready to play the Falcons.

We weren't. Atlanta won 27–14, and the game itself was uglier than that. They were handling us on both sides of the ball, and here's some numbers to prove it: By halftime, Atlanta led 13–0, had 245 total yards to our 25, and had 15 first downs to our 1.

With their quarterback, Bobby Hebert, lighting it up, our coaches seemed to feel our defense could not stop Atlanta. So in trying to keep up whenever we got the ball, they just kept sending in pass play after pass play. With two minutes left in the first half, I still had only one carry. I was furious, too. The last time I had one carry in a half, I played for Escambia High—and it had ticked me off then.

Sometimes bad days only get lousier. On one of the final plays of the first half, I tried sneaking through the line of scrimmage again, so Kosar could throw me a pass like the one I'd broken last week for 86 yards. But this time I ran into one of our pulling linemen. His knee struck my right thigh and I went straight to the ground. For one scary moment, I thought my leg was broken and I was done for the season.

I stayed on the turf, in sharp pain. I was able to stand up myself, but then I needed help to make it into our locker room. The X ray they took showed no broken bones. The doctor said I had deeply bruised my right quadriceps. I felt relieved, of course, that my leg wasn't broken. But the pain wouldn't go away, and I still thought my injury might be serious. I couldn't walk on my right leg, or even stand up on it. At minimum, I was definitely through for the afternoon.

Looking back, maybe we did go into Atlanta slightly cocky. That might be what Jimmy saw when none of our players did. In any case, Atlanta snapped our seven-game winning streak. At 7–3, we were tied again with the Giants for first place in the NFC East.

Unfortunately for me and my right quad, our next week was a short one. With Miami coming to Dallas for Thanksgiving, at first I didn't know if I could play. Some muscle bruises are so severe, nerves can be damaged. With this bruise, the doctor said he was concerned about flexibility. So to keep the muscle stretched, I had to sleep all Sunday night with my leg locked behind me in one position. First they put my leg in straps, then they bent it back so far my heel nearly touched my butt.

I barely slept, but it worked: On Monday morning I could walk again. I went right to our training room, where they continued to work on restoring my flexibility. Though

EMMITT SMITH

more progress was made, I still had enormous swelling around my thigh—so much swelling, in fact, we could not even see the muscles I have in my thighs. So the main goal from then on was reducing the swelling. This meant two solid days of ice packs. When Thursday finally came, I never wanted to see another ice pack.

So what fell from Dallas skies that Thanksgiving Day? Rain so cold it froze into ice. I couldn't escape the stuff.

Since I could now run without limping, at least for 25 yards or so, I also couldn't see missing such a big game. My teammates and I take pride in winning on Thanksgiving. Since my rookie year, we had won all three we'd played on the holiday. After coming out so lazy against Atlanta, we also saw the Miami game as a way to redeem ourselves.

I had never played football in nastier conditions. And while trying to run on ice with a bruised right leg, I carried just 16 times for 51 yards. Everyone seemed to be struggling that day—everyone except for two of our rookies. Lincoln Coleman, the runner who backed me up, carried 10 times for 57 yards. Kevin Williams, a threat to go all the way whenever he touches the ball, did exactly that on a 64-yard punt return for a touchdown.

Coming just twenty-seven seconds before halftime, Kevin's huge play gave us a 14–7 lead. Two field goals by Pete Stoyanovich made it 14–13 at the end of the third quarter. After James Washington forced a fumble, Darren Woodson recovered the ball at Miami's 30-yard line. At the moment, that play by James and Darren also looked huge. With less than four minutes left, 7 points here would put us ahead by 8. Even a field goal would make it 17–13, and Miami could win only by scoring a touchdown.

Neither scenario happened.

We couldn't get past the Miami 14, Eddie Murray missed from 32 yards, and the Dolphins still trailed 14–13. With 2:14 left to play, Steve DeBerg drove them all the way down to our 24, but the Dolphins ran out of time-outs with 15 seconds to play. As I stood on the sideline crossing my fingers, Pete Stoyanovich lined up for a 41-yard field goal. It all came down to this . . . and Jimmie Jones blocked it!

I thought, The game is over, the game is over!

Then I saw Leon Lett come out of nowhere, and I started screaming, "No, no, no!"

Everybody on our sideline was screaming, which is probably why Leon couldn't hear us. He went sliding into the ball and knocked it toward the goal line with his foot, and the Dolphins recovered at their 1-yard line. Leon hadn't realized it, but the ball was still live if he touched it. And given a second chance with three seconds left on the clock, Stoyanovich won the game with a 19-yard field goal.

Our second straight loss happened so fast, nobody could believe it. When I went looking for Leon after the game, I found him alone in the X-ray room. Just getting started in this league, Leon Lett is already one hell of a football player. Although he was in anguish, I knew Leon would forget this.

It also wasn't the time to make speeches, though. Looking him in the eye, I just said, "Don't worry about it, Leon."

When Leon didn't reply, I left him alone.

The media refused to. Man, they wouldn't let go. With

ten days before our next game, they just kept blasting away at Leon Lett. That really upset me. It's one thing for an athlete to get criticized in public; none of us *likes* this when it happens, but we also accept it as part of being a pro. But this reaction, this feeding frenzy, really went over the line. This went straight from critical to cruel. You want to know who was most out of control? Those sports-talk radio shows they have now in every big city. "Call in right now and tell us what you think of Leon Lett. Let's kick this man when he's down so we can boost our ratings." Some of these radio shows need to get a grip. That stuff can get really obnoxious.

With our record at 7–4, we had five games left to make our run for the playoffs. But our goal wasn't getting in as a wild card. We wanted to win the NFC East, so we could play our first-round game in Dallas. In order to do this, we'd probably have to win five in a row.

Calling us together that week at practice, Jimmy made the comical statement I mentioned before. "We've got five weeks of tough football in front of us," he said. "Now I can hang from my **** for the next five weeks, so we can get where we want to be. Can *you* guys hang from your **** for five weeks?"

Intriguing question. We'd start to answer it on December 6, when our next opponent, the Eagles, came into Dallas. The first time we played them, in the rain, I'd rushed for 237 yards. Now their defensive coordinator, Bud Carson, was vowing, "Emmitt Smith won't run for two hundred yards this time."

Bud Carson was right, but only by 28 yards. On *Monday*

THE EMMITT ZONE

Night Football, which I always enjoy playing on because I love center stage, I gained 172 yards on 23 carries. My longest run of the night was also my most important. With six minutes in the game and our 16–3 halftime lead cut to 16–10, I broke an inside handoff for 57 yards. Moose scored a few plays later and it was all over.

Our two-game losing streak ended, we won again at Minnesota, 37–20. It was an excellent game for our offense, because everybody played well. Troy completed 19 of 29 passes for 208 yards. Michael Irvin caught 8 of them for 125 yards. Eddie Murray kicked 3 long field goals, from 51, 52, and 46 yards. Although I started out slow, I ran for 104 yards and 1 short touchdown.

I did pay the price on one running play, though. The February before, I had played with the Vikings' Chris Doleman at the Pro Bowl. "I can't wait to play you guys next year," Chris told me in Hawaii. "You gotta come up to Minnesota, you know."

Yes, we did, and Chris took the occasion to knock the crap out of me. He grabbed me from behind on one of my runs, tore my helmet off, and made me bite my tongue. Good thing we had become friends at the Pro Bowl. He might have torn off my head.

Jimmy did some ripping himself after this game. Our offense had been nearly flawless against Minnesota, scoring on seven of our eight possessions. But in the game's final quarter and a half, our defense had let up a pair of touchdowns, and that's why Jimmy went off. I think Jimmy also saw something building: The Eagles had scored 17 the week before; the Vikings had just scored 20.

EMMITT SMITH

If the defense kept it up, Jimmy told the press, "it's going to be a very short season." Asked what he felt the defense had to improve on, Jimmy said, "Oh, a bunch of little things, like containing the passer, making tackles, playing off blocks."

Jimmy's postgame tirade worked—at least for the defense. In beating the New York Jets 28–7, our defense was dominating from start to finish, while our offense looked slick one moment and sloppy the next. And even though we won, it wasn't like us to play this way in December. Ordinarily, our team does more than win down the regular-season stretch. We also play our tightest football.

On December 24, two days before our next game against the Redskins, Troy Aikman signed his new contract with the Cowboys. I have to admit I was stunned when I heard the terms: $50 million over eight years, including an $11 million signing bonus.

Combined with the $2.5 million Troy would be paid as a salary, he would earn $13.5 this season alone. My entire four-year deal was worth $13.6 million.

That was only the contrast in terms of money. The process Troy and I went through was also like night and day. I had to complete the terms of my original contract and sit out our first two games, and I still got $4 million less than what I asked for. I also went through all that propaganda, with Jerry making statements about my value, and with people forming opinions on whether or not I was greedy. No—make that whether or not all modern athletes were greedy.

In retrospect, it was a joke. Because Jerry Jones never

put Troy through any of that. Troy's contract, in fact, was not even up yet. It still had two years to go, but Jerry agreed to a renegotiation. Just as some people in the league thought that he might, Jerry also did this deal behind the scenes. Some people even thought Troy's deal was done before mine, because Jerry knew I wouldn't sign if I learned exactly how fat Troy's contract was going to be.

I didn't know if that speculation was true, but the second part of it definitely was. If I somehow knew in September what Troy would sign for in December, I wouldn't have taken my deal. I would have accepted a gap, because Troy plays quarterback and I play running back. But not a gap as large as this one.

I guess that's why I felt so numb when I heard the news. I just kept saying it out loud: "Fifty million dollars, fifty million dollars, fifty million dollars."

My second reaction: What happened to the doggone salary cap? Jerry griped about it to me for weeks on end!

Just as Jerry did when I signed my contract, he announced Troy's at a Texas Stadium press conference. Again, there was no comparison. At my press conference, Jerry behaved like I ripped him off; Jerry was *beaming* at Troy's press conference. What happened to the guy who bragged about pinching pennies? For someone agreeing to pay out $50 million, Jerry Jones was in one hell of a mood.

So do I feel it was racial? In my opinion, even though quarterbacks make the biggest bucks in this league, Troy might never have gotten that money if he was a black quarterback.

Does that make Jerry Jones a racist? No, not necessarily. Maybe it just comes down to some people taking care of their own. If the Cowboys had a black owner, he might very well pay me better than he did Troy.

Let me close by stating the obvious: I have no hard feelings toward Troy over any of this. I didn't last December and I still don't. When Troy signed his deal I told him, "Congratulations." I meant it, too. Every man has the right to earn whatever he can.

■ ■ ■

On December 26, in a 38–3 rout against the Redskins, I gained 153 yards on 21 carries. My performance had nothing to do with my trying to make a statement. I just wanted to kick their butts.

The first game we played the Redskins, at RFK Stadium, I was still sitting out. After watching them destroy us 35–16, I found out the story behind the story. Without me in that game, the Redskins had two men all night on Michael Irvin. They were also talking trash, telling Michael, "Hey, boy, you're out here by yourself tonight. Your boy is back at home. What you gonna do now?" Michael was laughing when he told me this. But I went crazy. I told Mike, "I'll run the football down their damn throats!"

I was glad to play well against them, but the Redskins were also having a horrible season. After beating us in September, they won only three more games the rest of the season. Some people were shocked, because it was just two years since Washington had destroyed Denver in the Super Bowl. But that's how fast it can happen in this league. A veteran team gets older, its players get injured, it doesn't have enough young people to replace them. Before Jimmy Johnson came in and turned it around, the same thing had happened in Dallas.

With my 153 yards, I also took over the rushing lead for the first time. It wasn't over yet. We had one more regular-season game, against the Giants. But just being on top felt good after coming from so far behind.

"Yeah, but Barry Sanders was hurt," some people said. That was true. Barry injured his knee on Thanksgiving and missed several games. But Barry Foster and Rodney Hampton also got hurt that season. As for myself, I missed our first two games, came back to the Cowboys with hamstring problems, then carried once against Atlanta when I thought I broke my leg. I felt bad when I heard Barry Sanders went down; I don't like to see anybody get injured. But after working so hard that season, I was still proud of what I achieved.

On the Thursday before our game against the Giants, Jimmy Johnson went on ESPN. Jimmy said he was "intrigued" by the interest shown in him by the expansion Jacksonville Jaguars. Even though it made national news, I didn't think twice about Jimmy's comment. Jimmy had five years left on his contract with Jerry, and I didn't think Jerry would let him out. Also, most people *will* be intrigued when another organization regards them highly. I didn't take it to mean that Jimmy was leaving the Cowboys.

That's how most of our players saw it, I believe. From our point of view, the issue was minor. A bigger concern at the time was our offensive coordinator, Norv Turner. Jimmy Johnson, we figured, was staying put. But even before the playoffs began, we heard rumors that Norv would become head coach of the Redskins.

On Sunday, January 2, in New York, we did what championship teams do: Tuning out the distractions, we beat the Giants in overtime, 16–13. The win wasn't big—it was gigantic. It earned us the NFC East championship, a week off and home field advantage in the playoffs. From that point on, we all felt we'd repeat as Super Bowl champs. It wouldn't be easy, but nothing this season had been.

This was also the game when I separated my shoulder but still carried 32 times for 168 yards, caught 10 passes for 61 yards, and scored our only touchdown. Of my 229 total yards, 78 came after I injured my shoulder. Of the forty-two times I handled the ball, seventeen also came afterwards.

My performance seemed to move a lot of people, and the compliments started coming in. In a feature story, *Sports Illustrated* called it "determination on a national stage." The *Dallas Morning News* said it was "one of the best performances in Cowboys history." On national television, while the game was still being played, John Madden said something like, "If Troy Aikman is worth fifty million, then Emmitt Smith is worth that much too."

It was quite a day, and quite a regular season. My 168 yards against New York gave me a total of 1,486—and my third straight rushing title. In the history of the league, only Steve Van Buren, Earl Campbell, and Jim Brown had ever accomplished that feat. And I was the only runner to win the title after missing two games.

For the first time in my career, I led the NFL in total

yards from scrimmage, with 1,900. In another personal best, I also led the league with 5.3 yards per carry. As we closed out the regular season with five consecutive wins, I averaged 137.6 rushing yards per game, and for this I was named the NFC Offensive Player of the Month for that December, marking the third straight December I'd won that award. Then, to cap it all off, on January 10 I became the first Dallas Cowboy to win the NFL's Most Valuable Player award. Frankly, by then I expected to win it. But that didn't make the feeling any less sweet. Literally, the MVP was a dream come true.

Of all the wonderful praise and honors I received, one of the nicest moments happened in private, when my high school coach Dwight Thomas called me from Pensacola. Dwight said he'd watched the Giants game on TV and had never seen a more courageous performance. The pain he knew I was in had brought tears to his eyes, he said.

I choked up myself when Dwight said that. All these years, and my coach was still proud of me.

15
SUPER
AGAIN

mmediately after beating the Giants, we started the physical therapy on my right shoulder. So much blood and fluid had rushed into it, at first the swelling concealed my clavicle. To combat that, it was nothing but ice and rest for the first two days. Then the treatment changed to heat and motion. This would bring the blood flowing *in,* to start the healing. The new blood would also keep the old blood from clotting.

Throughout this accelerated rehab, I knew I'd play in our first-round game. Even if I wanted to, my teammates wouldn't stand for my sitting out. Led by Michael

Irvin, they kept telling me, "You're playing against the Packers. If you could play against the Giants, you can play this week."

As for any additional damage, I figured the worst I could do was a higher-grade separation. I was willing to take that risk in order to help us get to the Super Bowl. Let's throw it all in the Lord's hands, I thought, and then just see what happens.

On January 16 at Texas Stadium, we went into our game with the Packers confident and relaxed. Maybe we should have been more intense. While beating Green Bay, 27–17, we didn't perform like a Super Bowl team. Our defense stuffed their running game all day long, but our offense came out flat, and Green Bay led 3–0 after one quarter.

Thanks largely to Michael, Troy, Jay Novacek, and the pass-blocking that game, we finally cut loose in the next three quarters. Troy threw for 302 yards and 3 TDs, Mike had a personal playoff best of 9 catches for 126 yards, and Jay caught 6 balls and scored a touchdown.

Me? I was frustrated that I wasn't a bigger factor. After taking some early shots to my injured shoulder, I carried just 13 times for 60 yards. On one passing play in the third quarter, I used my shoulder to block their blitzing linebacker, Tony Bennett. It hurt so bad, I went down like I'd been shot. I struggled off the field, returned for two more plays, and called it a day. By then the game was in hand, and I was thinking ahead to our game with the 49ers.

Afterwards, the reporters wanted to know why we looked so imprecise. Were we *all* looking ahead to the 49ers? Even before we had this game won?

EMMITT SMITH

I probably shouldn't admit this, but I do think San Francisco was in the back of our minds. One day before we played the Packers on Sunday, San Francisco had played the Giants at Candlestick Park. I watched this shocking game at our hotel. Ricky Watters ran for 5 touchdowns, Steve Young hit 17 of 22 passes, their defense held the Giants to 41 yards rushing, and San Francisco drilled them, 44–3.

I saw that and said, "Oooh-weee. We will have a ball game next week in Dallas."

That's my point. We still hadn't played Green Bay.

On the positive side, seeing that game was a perfect wake-up call. If we did go in too cocky against the Packers, there was no chance of that now against San Francisco.

So why did Jimmy Johnson proceed to stir things up? Because that's what Jimmy does. The man is many things, but never dull.

The Thursday night before our game, Jimmy was listening to a show on sports-talk radio. Hearing all the back-and-forth about who would win, Jimmy surprised the station by calling in himself. His second surprise was predicting a Dallas victory. "We will win the game," Jimmy guaranteed. "You can put it in three-inch headlines."

When it made the morning papers, I just smiled and shook my head. I also thought: It might not be a bad thing. Nobody knows us better than he does. If Jimmy thinks we'll win, we probably will.

But George Seiffert thought Jimmy was out of line. The coach of the 49ers, he said Jimmy must "have big cojones" to make a comment like that. I smiled when I heard that too. The fun was beginning, and it was just Friday.

THE EMMITT ZONE

On Sunday at Texas Stadium, moments before the NFC Championship Game, the 49ers were obviously still angry. Though not really known for talking trash, they seemed to be looking for confrontation. And they didn't even wait until the game got started. After our public-address announcer introduced them first, they stood in front of *our* goalpost blocking our way. The fight this nearly started set the tone for the day.

Against the Packers we'd featured the passing game, partly because we thought we could throw on them, partly because my shoulder was still banged up. This week my shoulder felt stronger, our opponent was better, and our coaches thought I needed to have more impact. To involve me from the start, they designed a few new pass plays. Nothing fancy, just some short and safe routes to get the ball in my hands. In watching the films of the 49ers, our coaches had noticed something they felt they could exploit. When other teams sent running backs out for passes, San Francisco's linebackers covered them one-on-one. If the same thing happened this week, our coaches thought we could burn them.

They tested their theory midway through the first quarter. With no score in the game, we had a third down and 6 at our own 29. I caught a pass from Troy in the flat, faked out the linebacker waiting for me, eluded another defender who tried a leg whip, and raced 28 yards for our first big play. Later that drive, I ran 5 yards off-tackle to make it 7–0.

But after San Francisco scored to tie it 7–7, I made a horrible play on our next series. At the San Francisco 4,

Troy faked a pitchout to me running right, then quickly handed off inside to Moose. He scored with ease, but no thanks to me. The fake I made stunk; I actually turned around and watched the play. Good thing the blocking was perfect. I don't know what the hell I was thinking about.

On our offensive series after that one, it was San Francisco's turn to make a mental mistake. Just as they had the year before at Candlestick Park—in that season's NFC Championship Game—they blew an assignment badly and I scored an easy touchdown. On a circle route out of the backfield, I caught the ball over the middle, where normally people get blasted. This time nobody even covered me. I was so wide open Troy couldn't miss me. When he didn't, my 11-yard TD made it 21–7, Cowboys.

Five minutes later, we led 28–7 when Troy hit Jay Novacek with a 19-yard pass. Our offense had put on a clinic in the first half: four touchdowns in five possessions, 273 total yards. Our defense did a job too. Against an explosive team that had just scored 44 points, our defense held them to a single first-half touchdown. For the whole game, our defense would allow San Francisco just 84 yards on the ground.

Sprinting into our locker room leading 28–7, everyone talked about not letting down. Then our offensive linemen did exactly that. It didn't last long, only one series, but the damage was done. After playing a brilliant first half—14 of 18 for 177 yards and 2 touchdowns—Troy got knocked out of the game.

It happened on our first series of the third quarter. First, I carried the ball for no gain. That play looked like a jailbreak, there were so many 49ers busting through. As Troy dropped back to pass the following play, the defense poured through again. Troy escaped the first two 49ers, but then ran into a third: 300-pound defensive end Dennis Brown, whose knee struck Troy in the head.

Troy stood up slowly, grabbing his head, but I didn't think he was hurt badly. Returning to our huddle, he called the next play correctly, and also ran it correctly. After we punted, our offense came off together. That's when I saw how far out of it Troy really was. Ordinarily when a player sniffs ammonia, his head snaps back and his eyes blink. Troy looked like he'd just sniffed water. No reaction at all.

That ended Troy's afternoon, and we later found out he suffered a concussion. He spent that hazy night at a hospital in Dallas.

Bernie Kosar played well in relief, with 83 yards passing and a 42-yard TD to Alvin Harper. That made it Dallas 35, San Francisco 14 with about three minutes left in the third quarter. Jimmy decided to pull me out of the game. After 88 yards rushing, 85 yards receiving, and 2 touchdowns, I took off my pads, sat on the bench, and started icing my shoulder.

Our 38–21 victory felt fantastic, but it wasn't time yet for a big celebration. Next stop was Atlanta, to defend our Super Bowl crown against the Bills.

■ ■ ■

On the Monday after playing the 49ers, our plane touched down at Hartsfield Atlanta International Airport. We had to get out there quickly, because there was no bye week this year before the Super Bowl. The NFL, instead, had given each team two byes in the regular season.

On paper, at least, I felt this helped the Bills. With no week off before the Super Bowl, my shoulder and Troy's head had less time to heal. Jimmy had less time to prepare for the Bill's no-huddle offense. Because look what happened the Super Bowl before, when Jimmy had two weeks instead of one. Our defense forced 9 turnovers and we won 52–17. It's a sports cliché, but it's true: Give a great coach like Jimmy extra preparation, and he'll almost always beat you.

Not having the bye week also meant something else: Going into my second Super Bowl, I was feeling freaked out by the *Sports Illustrated* jinx.

For the second straight year, I made their cover after we beat San Francisco. This year, however, I didn't have a bye week to protect me. As we were driving to dinner one night in Atlanta, Werner Scott and Larry Lundy gave me the news. They're my marketing guys, so naturally they were excited. I was aghast. "Oh my goodness!" I said. "You guys do everything in your power to get me off that cover! I don't want anyone saying I'm the reason we lost."

I couldn't help myself. The jinx had just hit *again* the previous week. A few days after Joe Montana made *Sports Illustrated*'s cover, his Chiefs lost to the Bills in the AFC Championship Game. Joe Montana, the quarterback god? "I'm serious," I said. "I don't want to be on that cover."

Werner and Larry laughed and said it was too late. Better adjust my attitude, they suggested.

Good suggestion. "Forget the jinx," I started telling the

press. "I've done other things first before anyone else. I'll be the first one now to beat the jinx."

My pre–Super Bowl highlight was meeting Michael Jordan. The night of Magic Johnson's Super Bowl party, the Hard Rock Cafe was jammed with close to five hundred people. As I walked inside the front door, I heard people screaming, "Michael, Michael!" I turned around and there was the man himself. I'd already met Magic and Barkley and Dominique. But never Michael J.

I said, "Hey, Michael!"

He said, "Hey, what's up, Emmitt?"

We shook hands and embraced, and I told him what a pleasure this was for me. Just before we both fought through the crowd, Michael said, "We should play golf sometime."

"Definitely," I said. "I'll be more than happy to play golf with you any day you want."

It hasn't happened yet, but I hope it does. It would be thrilling for me to play golf with Michael Jordan. In fact, my goal is to be the Michael Jordan of football. Michael's monstrous fame I could do without, but I'd sure like to equal his monstrous performance.

Wednesday at practice we found out Troy was still hurting. In the huddle, he was barely moving his head. When someone asked what was wrong, Troy said he had a bad headache. I felt for him, but I wasn't concerned about his performance on Sunday. Headaches or not, Troy looked sharp as ever in practice that week. I also knew how determined this guy was. His back, his shoulder, his hamstring, and now his head—on and off all season, Troy had played hurt.

EMMITT SMITH

In addition to Troy's readiness for the game, the hype centered on Buffalo's three straight Super Bowl losses. Some people were disappointed to see them back this year, but I felt Buffalo had earned the right to be there. And I was glad they had. Still disputing my contract with Jerry Jones, I'd missed our game against Buffalo in September. They not only beat us in Dallas that afternoon, they double-covered our wideouts and dared us to run. So now, all week in Atlanta, I used that first Buffalo game as a motivating tool: Yeah, Bills, you did it to us in Dallas, but this time you have to deal with me.

On Sunday, January 30, 1994, around 5 P.M. at the beautiful Georgia Dome, we won the coin toss and chose to receive. I thought: Good, let's get it on. We'll score on these guys the first time we get the ball. Then we won't only win, we'll blow them away.

Wrong. One thousand percent wrong. We came out stale, lacking emotion. How could we let that happen in such a big game? It's hard to pin down. Because of what happened in last year's Super Bowl, we possibly came into this game too self-assured. But give Buffalo credit: They whipped us those first thirty minutes, especially their defense.

The first time I carried the ball our opening drive, I swept to my left and tried hurling one Buffalo tackler. Bruce Smith came charging up and flipped me into the air. I crashed back down for no gain, and the Buffalo fans in Atlanta got excited. As I was standing up, another Buffalo player jumped in my face: "Yeah! Yeah! It's gonna be like this all day!"

Eddie Murray bailed us out with a field goal. Then their

kicker, Steve Christie, nailed one from 54 yards. Though kicking inside a dome, without any wind or elements, this was still a great kick, one which I never thought he'd make. But Christie showed us all how strong his leg really is.

Our offense struggled again our second series, actually going backwards this time by 2 yards. Buffalo's coaches had scouted us well. Their defense was stuffing the lead draw to me, which is one of our most productive plays. It's designed to look like a pass, so the defense rushes upfield and I can burst right by them. But the Bills were smart and experienced. They were sitting back and reading, waiting to see if Troy slipped me the ball.

Eddie Murray's second field goal put us ahead 6–3. Then Jim Kelly got hot, nitpicking us to death with his short, hard, accurate passes. Again, Buffalo's coaches had done their homework. Our defense is very difficult to beat long, but some teams have had success by pecking away. This particular drive, capped by Thurman Thomas's 4-yard TD run, went 80 yards and 17 plays. Seventeen plays! That entire first half, I knew our defense was on the field too long. For that, I thought our offense was partly to blame: We couldn't sustain a drive to give them some rest.

With the Bills leading 10–6 in the second quarter, we punted *again* on our fourth possession. This time, our linemen and I came back to the sideline grumbling. We felt the Bills were taking the fight to us. We wanted to play more physical football. Meaning we wanted to keep the ball on the ground.

"What are we doing, Emmitt?" our offensive linemen

were saying to me on our bench. "How come we're not running the ball? Why are we letting them bring it to us?"

After Buffalo also punted, nothing really changed on our next drive. We mostly continued passing, and for a while it worked. But on first and 10 from Buffalo's 37, Troy looked for Alvin Harper and missed him. Riley Odoms intercepted, then ran the ball 41 yards to Buffalo's 47. It turned into a big play, because Buffalo took over with one minute left in the half, and Kelly quickly drove them to our 12-yard line. With a first and 10, a touchdown here would put them up 17–6.

I took a deep breath—and watched our defense come up with a monumental stop. On Buffalo's next three downs, they gained 1 yard, and had to settle for a field goal. Knowing it could've been worse, we went into halftime losing 13–6.

"We MUST pick it up in the second half. More big plays! We need more big plays!"

That's what our players were saying as we piled into our locker room. I didn't sense any doubt, though—just what seemed to me like a deeper resolve. The rings. We wanted the rings.

Jimmy Johnson was cool. Intense but cool.

"We have to get back out there and be more aggressive," he told us. "Wrap up on tackles, and get into Kelly's face. I want to see some balls batted down this half. Offensively, Troy needs time to throw the ball. And we have to establish the run."

That's what I wanted to hear. And when Jimmy finished, Norv Turner walked over to me. He asked how my shoulder felt. I told him fine. Then I think we both knew what I was about to say.

"Norv, I need the ball in my hands more," I said.

"How do you want me to get it to you?" he said.

"It doesn't matter. Just *get* it to me."

"Okay. We'll try a few new plays in the running game, see how they work."

One of those plays was called Power Right. But I'll tell you about that a bit later on.

To open the third quarter, Buffalo had the ball and its 13–6 lead. On only their third play, Thurman Thomas ran into Leon Lett. I never saw Leon cause the fumble, but I did see James Washington pick up the ball. As James took off running, I never thought he'd make it into the end zone—too many Bills in his way. But as James kept cutting and cutting back, I started jumping up and down. James went all the way in from 46 yards, making it 13–13 and changing the game's direction.

James had pumped me up so high, I could hardly wait for my turn. But I had to: Eddie Murray was kicking off to the Bills again. When our defense quickly stopped them, our offense ran out for the first time that half.

Norv Turner kept his word. He gave me the ball.

As our offense finally put together a drive, I carried 7 out of 8 plays, for 61 of our 64 yards. Most of them came on what we call Power Right, one of the running plays Norv talked about implementing at halftime. Power Right basically works the same way it sounds: From his spot at left tackle, Nate Newton pulls to the right. Right guard Kevin Gogan and right tackle Erik Williams both block down. If there's anybody left standing in the hole, Moose takes him out. I follow those four big hosses and look for some running room.

First and 10 from our 36, I ran 9 yards on a Power Right.

Second and 1, I ran a slant for 3 yards.

First and 10 at our 48, I thought we'd pass. But Norv stayed with Power Right and I went for 9 yards.

Second and 1, I ran Power Right for 7 yards.

First and 10 at the Buffalo 36, I ran 14 yards on another Power Right, and now I'm coming back to the huddle screaming. Screaming to my teammates on the sideline, screaming to my teammates in the huddle, screaming so loud I'm sure the Bills can hear me, but right now I really don't care. I'm screaming, "Yeah! This is what I'm talking about! This is what I'm talking about! Give it to me again! Give it to me again!"

First and 10 at the Buffalo 14, Norv Turner stayed stuck on Power Right. I went for another 4 yards on my sixth straight carry.

That's when all the running and screaming caught up with me. Winded, I went to the sideline for one play. Troy hit Moose with a 3-yard screen pass, to make it third and 3 at the Buffalo 15. The score was still tied at 13.

Power Right. I scored a 15-yard touchdown to put us up 20–13.

I still love watching that drive when I see it today. Normally, I don't watch myself in old games. But I put that Super Bowl drive in my VCR a lot. I'll never forget it as long as I live.

THE EMMITT ZONE

On the first play of the fourth quarter, James Washington crushed what was left of Buffalo's hopes. Stepping in front of Don Beebe at the last moment, James picked off Jim Kelly's pass and returned it to the Buffalo 36. Eight plays later I scored a 1-yard TD, making it 27–13, Cowboys. There was still 9 minutes left, but I thought the game was pretty much over by then. Our defense was putting incredible heat on Kelly.

Eddie Murray's field goal made the final score Dallas 30, Buffalo 13. In the second half, with the Super Bowl on the line, our team had scored 24 unanswered points.

Right after Eddie's field goal, a lady from Disney walked up to me on our sideline. For my 30 carries, 2 touchdowns, and 132 yards, I had been named the Super Bowl MVP. This was another joyous moment I'll never forget. After winning the regular-season MVP, I'd won it in the Super Bowl as well. I was also the first player ever to win the NFL rushing title and Super Bowl MVP in the same season. But as I told the reporters after the game, "I wish there was some way they could have given coawards, so James Washington could have gotten something."

I wasn't trying to be diplomatic. In addition to his 46-yard TD—the single biggest play of the Super Bowl— and his key interception in the fourth quarter, James had forced a fumble in the first half. He also led all players with 11 solo tackles.

Before going into our locker room, I spent some time on the field with my goddaughter Kendra. There was so much commotion down there, she looked scared to death, so I held her hand tightly while I looked for Thurman

Thomas. Thurman had fumbled twice, the second one turning into James Washington's long TD run. I spotted Thurman and gave him a hug, told him to keep his head up, reminded him what a great ball player he was. Thurman said into my shoulder, "Congratulations." I told him "Thank you" and squeezed him harder.

Once I made it into our locker room, I was one of the last to leave, maybe because this year's win felt even more special than last year's. On top of the fact that we lost our first two games, more people played hurt this season. As defending Super Bowl champs, we all felt more pressure. Everybody was watching, and every team in the league was gearing up to stop us. That keeps a ball club sharp, but can also be exhausting.

Later that evening I felt too wired to sleep. But who felt like sleeping anyway? As soon as I arrived at our hotel, a group of my family and friends were waiting for me. By then, I'd already decided I wouldn't play in the Pro Bowl. It was only four weeks to this day that I'd separated my shoulder. After 30 carries against the Bills, it was banged up pretty good.

Since I knew I wouldn't be playing a football game that week, I ordered a bunch of food and champagne for my family and friends. My goddaughter Kendra tried staying up all night too, but she finally fell dead asleep while all the adults were still going strong. As for me? I stayed up until four or five in the morning. Stretching it out for all it was worth.

16
LOOKING DOWNFIELD

ust three days after the Super Bowl, the franchise received its first postseason blow. Norv Turner, as expected, accepted the job as head coach of the Washington Redskins. When I read about it, I felt the same way I did when Dave Wannstedt left Dallas: extremely pleased for Norv, and disappointed for us. I've played football all my life, and Norv knows offense as well as anyone I've encountered. He's also meant a great deal to my own development. If not for Norv and the opportunity he gave me, I might still be searching for recognition. Thank you for everything, Norv.

About two weeks later, in mid-February, I flew to Birmingham, Alabama, where Dr. James Andrews evaluated my shoulder. One of the top orthopedic surgeons in the world, Dr. Andrews once operated on Bo Jackson's hip. Just the previous June, he had performed back surgery on Troy Aikman. It was Troy who recommended Dr. Andrews to me.

After looking at X rays and testing my shoulder for strength, Dr. Andrews told me that I required surgery. My clavicle was so unstable, he said, he could touch the bone and make it bounce up and down. I didn't need any prodding once I heard that.

But two weeks later, the night before my surgery, I was a nervous wreck. I'd never been under the knife, and the nurse was explaining the procedure to me. After cutting through the muscle to reach the bone, they'd cut that bone by about an inch, press it back down, and strap it in place. But what really freaked me out was the tube they'd stick in my throat, in order to help me breathe while I was unconscious. That was the part of the plan that made my heart race.

To my relief, the tube was already gone when I woke up. A few minutes later, Dr. Andrews walked in and told me he was pleased. He also said it was a good thing we went ahead and did this. My shoulder was even more damaged than he could tell from the X rays. After making his incisions, he'd seen that the tip of my bone was gnawed to pieces. He thought it came from the hits I took—once I was already injured. Each time the loose bone moved up and down, another piece scraped away.

I still had no regrets about playing hurt, though. If it

EMMITT SMITH

happened again, I'd do the same thing. My performance helped us get our second ring.

The point of having the surgery so quickly, in early March, was for me to be ready when camp began in July. So the very next morning after my operation, I was already doing light rehab. In the next several weeks I slowly picked up the pace, and today my shoulder feels as strong as it ever has. It's ready to rumble, and so am I.

■　■　■

The third week of March, I picked up the morning paper and found a bombshell inside it. This is essentially what I read:

The night before, during the NFL meetings in Orlando, Jimmy was having a drink with some former Cowboy coaches. When Jerry came by and made a toast, they didn't ask him to sit down. Later that evening, Jerry apparently spoke to the press about firing Jimmy. Jerry said he might replace Jimmy with Barry Switzer, adding that five hundred coaches would have won the Super Bowl with the team we had this season.

My initial reaction: This doesn't sound good at all. Jimmy will be furious when he hears this.

He was, of course, and I didn't blame him. Even if Jerry was joking, or tipsy, this was Jimmy's livelihood he was talking about. And even if Jerry said his comments were off the record, he understands how the press works. He had to know his remarks would make all the papers.

So why did Jerry do it? Maybe he just wasn't thinking intelligently. Maybe he was just miffed that he wasn't asked to sit down. On the other hand, maybe Jerry was more calculating than that. With all the conflicts he and Jimmy already had, maybe Jerry wanted to outrage him, so Jimmy would resign and Jerry could bring in Switzer. I mean, look how fast Jerry had Switzer signed to a contract—the very next day after Jimmy said he was gone. Maybe it was just happenstance.

The day after Jerry made his statement, Jimmy left the NFL meetings in Orlando. The rest of that week, Jimmy and Jerry made comments through the press. On Saturday Jimmy arrived in Pensacola.

Jimmy flew in to speak at my football camp. This was my first in Pensacola, but I'd been holding a camp the past three summers in Dallas. I always try to make sure the kids have fun, but I also don't mislead them. Before we get started I ask them why they came. If I hear any kids say, "To get autographs," I tell them, "Well, you're at the wrong camp. This camp is all about teaching and learning. When you leave here, we want you to understand more about this game. And we want you to play it better than ever before." I also talk about discipline and commitment, and how important it is for them to set goals—the things I learned from Dwight Thomas when I was a kid.

At some of my camps in Dallas, Michael and Troy and Bill Bates have worked with the kids. Among others at this first one in Pensacola, Thurman Thomas, Warren Moon, Tony Dorsett, James Washington, Cornelius Bennett, Alexander Wright, Russell Maryland, Mitchell Price, Eugene Lockhart, Tony Smith, Lincoln Coleman, and Alfredo Roberts were all nice enough to participate. So was Jimmy Johnson, whose presence meant a lot to me. With everything going on, I'd have understood if he canceled.

But Jimmy seemed happy that morning, even relaxed. And even though he was there to give a speech, he jumped right in and took part in the drills. During one drill for the kids who play running back, Tony Dorsett was standing near the sideline, making the kids run just inside or outside him. Jimmy got all hyped up and ran to where Tony was standing. "Come on, Tony," Jimmy said, "you gotta get in there and do it like this!"

Just playing around, I walked over and grabbed Jimmy by his shoulder. "Coach, you better come on over here with me," I said. "I don't want anything to happen to you. Now, if Jerry was running the football, then I'd let you stand here, and you two could do the drill!"

Jimmy smiled, but underneath it I saw how ticked off he really was. Letting the other guys run the drill, Jimmy and I walked a few feet away. He tried to speak, but he was so mad that nothing left his mouth.

"I know, I know," I said. "Don't even worry about it, Coach."

Jimmy flew back to Dallas after he spoke to the kids. Once he was gone, I was approached by some writers who covered my camp. They wanted to know how I felt about Jimmy's situation.

"I'm behind Jimmy all the way," I said. "Fire Jimmy— fire me too."

This last sentence was only a figure of speech. I never thought Jerry Jones would fire Jimmy. If anything, as I said, I thought maybe he might try provoking Jimmy into resigning.

When my quote was printed in Dallas and Pensacola, and later all over the country, some people thought I was speaking in anger. But I wasn't angry at all when I made that comment. And I never thought seriously about "retiring." I was just showing my loyalty. I'd seen the strain myself that Jimmy was under.

On Monday afternoon, Jimmy and Jerry met to sort out their future. I flew back to Dallas that night, and nothing had been resolved. With Jimmy and Jerry meeting again in the morning, I felt, it could go either way.

I went to our complex on Tuesday morning, but it was so packed with cameras and reporters, I went to play golf. On the fourth or fifth hole, someone told me Jimmy was leaving the Cowboys. For a moment I felt stunned, but then I just kept playing golf. I didn't want to believe it, and I wouldn't believe it until I saw for myself. Not with all the gossip that week in Dallas.

Later that afternoon, watching the news in my apartment, I said to myself, "This is crazy. It doesn't make any sense. Jimmy's the best coach in football. He just led us to our second straight Super Bowl. What exactly did he do wrong?"

As I kept watching, they ran some tape of the press conference from that day. Jimmy and Jerry were acting like buddies.

Something's not right here, I thought. This is a farce.

Within a few days, I heard the details of Jimmy's going-away deal. Jerry not only ripped up the last five years of his contract—making Jimmy a free man—he also gave him a large cash bonus. That's probably why Jimmy acted so mellow that day.

I don't know what went on between them in private, or if Jimmy's resignation was truly a mutual choice. But I do believe Jimmy was already getting fed up, and that this last event in Orlando pushed him over the edge. Even before this, there was the 1992 holdout of eight of our veteran players, including Michael Irvin, one of Jimmy's favorites, who didn't sign until three days before the season. There was my contract impasse last year, when Jimmy evidently tried interceding, and Jerry basically told him, "It's none of your business." Just this past January, there was Jerry's claim that he could coach the Cowboys.

I will give Jerry credit for two things, though: his business mind and his judgment in hiring. It was Jerry who brought in Jimmy, the biggest single reason the Cowboys got turned around. But Jerry and Jimmy, unfortunately, have parted ways, and several of last year's free agents have also left Dallas. As for the Cowboys still here, I know we'll all continue playing our hearts out. But once our next contracts are up, who knows? If we think our owner cares more about ego and money than winning, this team may still be destroyed from the top someday.

As for Barry Switzer, he seems as if he cares about his players. He seems to have the energy and the drive. Obviously it's early, but I think Barry is doing just fine so far. Jimmy is working at Fox in the broadcast booth, but I think he'll be back in coaching fairly soon. And I think it will be in the NFL.

THE EMMITT ZONE

■ ■ ■

Since I'm only twenty-five, I hope most of my life is still in front of me. Because I have plenty of dreams I want to pursue. I think everybody should dream, no matter how young or old they are. If you can't dream it then how can you make it real?

Having played only four NFL seasons, I have not yet achieved what some of the all-time greats have. But I think of those guys a lot: Walter Payton, Jim Brown, Tony Dorsett, Eric Dickerson. Before my career is over, I hope to make the kind of sports history they did. Then I want the new running backs to think about chasing me.

Down the road I'd like to make the Hall of Fame, and also the Dallas Cowboys' Ring of Honor. And I hope to surpass Walter Payton's career rushing record of 16,726 yards. With 5,699 yards after four seasons, I'd have to average about 1,500 yards for the next eight years. To even have a chance, I need to stay healthy, to continue playing behind great offensive lines, and to keep my own competitive fires stoked. If I do all that and still fall short, I won't be disappointed. I'll have had a hell of a run.

My future after football?

I plan to play golf at beautiful, challenging courses. I plan to travel around and check out my friends. I also still want the feeling I get from football—the feeling of working hard and seeing results. So I'll probably take off my pads and put on a business suit. I'm already doing some business now, and I want to continue growing. I mean that financially and also in terms of my skills. Whatever the arena, I want to perform.

EMMITT SMITH

My college degree is also important to me. I need eighteen more credits, so I'm only about one packed semester away. But my education won't stop once I earn my degree. There is so much to learn out there, and I haven't scratched the surface.

One day I'd like to get married, and I want my wife to be independent, to have her own convictions and aspirations. Women like that are more interesting to me. As for children, I definitely want them. I'd like at least one boy and one girl, and I don't care if they ever play sports. Sometimes I'll probably spoil them, but I won't be a pushover. My children will do chores. They will respect their elders and get their education. Someday they'll have to grow up and fend for themselves. They'll need to have some character to draw on.

Most of all, I will try to love my kids the way my family loved me. If I can accomplish that, my children will be as lucky as I have been. So I want to sign off by saying thanks to my family. Thanks for your love and guidance and optimism and strength. I hope you're as proud of me as I am of you.

INDEX